PRACTICAL GUIDE FOR CIO, SECOND EDITION

Your Compass for Navigating the World of IT Leadership

Radu Spataru

Contents

Why This Book?
Who is This Book For?
Chapter 1. Your journey as CIO / Head of IT
  1.1 Assess Current Status
  1.2 Create Your Strategy
  1.3 Create and Manage Your Strategy Execution Roadmap
  1.4 Manage Your Internal and External Processes
  1.5 Build Your Team
  1.6 Manage Technology
  1.7 Manage IT Budget
Chapter "Vs". My Vision and Values.
Chapter "C". Culture
Chapter 2. Assessment of the status – AS IS.
Chapter 3. Building Your Strategy
  3.1 Discover Business Strategy
  3.2 Build IT Strategy
  3.3 Present Strategy to the CEO and Business Departments
Chapter 4. Create and Manage Your Strategy Execution Roadmap
Chapter 5. Management of Your Internal and External Processes
  5.1 Service Level Agreements (SLAs)
  5.2 Information Security
  5.3 Change Management Process
  5.4 Roadmap Process and Related Elements
  5.5 Tools for Roadmap and Task Management
  5.6 Monitoring and Support Processes
  5.7 Disaster Recovery and Business Continuity
Chapter 6. Build Your Team
  6.1 Hiring Process
  6.2 Manage Continuous Learning - Hard and Soft Skills

6.3 Implement Salary Structure and Career Path.

6.4 Implement Motivational Systems

6.5 Manage properly Communication and Meetings

Chapter 7. Manage Technology

7.1 Manage the Borders of IT

7.2 Have Key Technical Knowledge Inside Your Team.

7.3 Selection of Proper Architecture/Technical Solution

7.4 Monitoring Tools and Processes Are Mandatory

7.5 Reporting and BI - Manage Them Properly

7.6 Information Security

7.7 Manage your IT KPIs

Chapter 8. Manage IT Budget

8.1 Budget Planning

8.2 Budget Review

8.3 IT Budget Domains

8.4 The Strategic Essence of IT Spending

Chapter 9. Choosing the Right Project Management Methodology

9.1 What is the Waterfall methodology?

9.2 What is Agile methodology?

9.3 Which Methodology to use?

Chapter 10. CIO Checklist (bonus chapter)

Conclusion

Abbreviations used in this book.

List of Diagrams and Tables

References

Why This Book?

Every day, we encounter stories of failure: numerous startup businesses collapse, and established enterprise companies fail in many cases —ranging from product launches to data protection incidents.

> "APPROXIMATELY 75% OF VENTURE-BACKED STARTUPS FAIL. THE NUMBER IS DIFFICULT TO PIN DOWN, AND SOME ESTIMATES SUGGEST IT COULD BE EVEN HIGHER."
>
> ELIZABETH POLLMAN (STUDY ABOUT REASONS OF STARTUP FAILURE)

These failures often arise from a variety of reasons: running out of cash, internal team issues, product development or business model flaws, fierce competition, a lack of market need, or changing circumstances.

Confronted with these stories, we might react by:
- Feeling fearful - "What if that happens to me?"
- Becoming overconfident - "That won't happen to me."
- Reflecting critically - "What are the common factors in these failures, and how can we identify and address our mistakes before they lead to disaster?"

It prompts us to question our actions and their effectiveness. Are we genuinely focused on making the right decisions and taking the necessary steps to progress, perform well, and rectify our mistakes?

Many failures are tied to IT projects and products, often involving teams of various sizes. This underappreciated fact among many IT leaders prompted the creation of this book.

The primary goal of this book is outlined in detail in the following pages, but in essence - I aim to empower today's leaders and managers. By doing things right today, we pave the way for a brighter tomorrow, marked by successful teams, projects, companies, and personal lives.

A Brief Overview of My Working Experience

Over the years, I have garnered extensive experience across various IT domains, including administration, database management, and support engineering. My career has been a journey of continual growth and a deep-seated desire to drive positive change.

Transitioning from an expert to roles such as Team Leader, IT Manager, Project Manager, and eventually CIO (Chief Information Officer) / CTO (Chief Technical Officer), each new position brought not only better remuneration and conditions but also new challenges. This evolution required a fundamental shift in mindset; expertise in processes was no longer sufficient. New management responsibilities beckoned, including budgeting, leading teams, resolving conflicts, and more.

Despite having a job description, I sought a comprehensive understanding of my responsibilities. How could I contribute to the company's improvement and stability? How could I lead a motivated team that recognized their role in the broader business strategy beyond their individual tasks?

With nearly two decades of experience in Technology Management, I felt compelled to distill the insights I've gathered into clear, actionable guidance for others. This book is designed to be a valuable resource for any CIO or Head of IT, offering a solid foundation for mastering the complexities of their roles and driving towards excellence and team success.

I trust that this book will prove invaluable in guiding you through the complexities of Technology Management. When I embarked on my journey years ago, I yearned for a comprehensive list of elements that could serve as a reliable guide, ensuring that no crucial aspect was overlooked.

All the real-life cases presented are genuine, with minor modifications made solely to eliminate any confidential elements. My primary objective was to share authentic examples from real-life situations without causing harm to anyone.

Building a foundation rooted in practical experience is essential, and that is precisely what I aim to provide.

Who is This Book For?

This book is crafted for a diverse audience, regardless of their current role within the IT sphere. Throughout the guide, I use the term "CIO" interchangeably with IT Manager, IT Leader, IT Director, Head of IT, or CTO (in some scenarios). The use of "CIO" is meant to broadly encompass these varied positions.

Stepping into the role of a CIO introduces distinct challenges, shaped by the specific circumstances you encounter:

- **New Company, New IT Team:** Perhaps you're joining as a new member of the IT team within a newly established company, or you might be the very first IT employee there! Key questions emerge: Where do I start? How do I lay a solid foundation for the IT team and/or department?
- **Company Growth, Expanded IT Needs:** In a company that's scaling up, the once small and efficient IT team now needs to expand. This growth phase demands careful planning, team development, establishment of rules and processes, delegation, and effective leadership, regardless of whether you already have a team with the necessary expertise.
- **Transitioning as an Incoming CIO:** Taking over from a previous CIO, whether promoted internally or hired externally, presents its unique set of challenges. You might inherit valuable resources and insights, or you might be starting from scratch.

No matter the scenario, a common necessity exists — the need for a clear starting point and a defined destination. This book aims to provide you with the initial directions, offering insights and strategies to commence your role as a CIO successfully, establish and manage a resilient IT team, and create an IT environment that benefits both the company and its individuals.

Additionally, this book offers valuable insights:

- For seasoned CIOs looking for a new perspective on evaluating their responsibilities.

- For IT professionals aiming to rise to (or gain a better understanding of) the roles of Chief Information Officers (CIOs) or Heads of IT departments.

Regardless of your current role, your situation within the company, or the state of the company itself, this book is designed to guide you through your journey, serving as a comprehensive navigator and handbook for becoming a successful CIO.

Chapter 1. Your journey as CIO / Head of IT

This chapter provides a summary of the topics we will cover in this book. In each subsequent chapter, we will delve deeper into each subject and explore real-life cases. Throughout the book, you'll find various templates that can be used immediately.

In the preceding section, various scenarios were outlined to illustrate the diverse situations in which one might assume the role of a CIO. While these situations are not exhaustive, the following steps are imperative for any CIO to establish a robust foundation and secure sustained support from the business and toward the business.

These constitute the practical fundamental principles for every manager overseeing IT (each step outlined here will be comprehensively explained in the upcoming chapters).

> "TODAY'S IT LEADERS NEED TO BE BUSINESS LEADERS FIRST, WITH A STRONG UNDERSTANDING OF THE ORGANIZATION'S STRATEGIC GOALS, MARKET CONTEXT, AND BUSINESS PROCESSES." JILL DYCHE

Real-life story: starting position of Technology Director in a new company.

I assumed the role of leading the Technical Department (role like CIO) in a dynamic company, responsible for delivering and managing software products as part of our business. Despite the team's size not being extensive, the company's success depended entirely on the Technical Department's delivery, quality, and overall efficiency.

Upon my arrival, after a short time, I noticed the following difficult situation: the teams were trapped in repetitive cycles, tackling Roadmap projects sequentially, resolving incidents, and attempting optimizations without substantial success.

Senior developers were often split between incident resolution and projects lacking clear formalization, leading to persistent rework.

The consequences were impacting the whole company: a decline in SLA (Service Level Agreement), incidents with long solution time, and stormy dissatisfaction on the Business side. Business projects, too, were adversely impacted by the focus on incidents, generating additional discontent.

This loop resembled a dead end, where individual tasks were completed, but overall dissatisfaction prevailed, reflecting poorly on the company's results.

Adding complexity, the evolving technology landscape demanded teams to explore new trends and adopt the latest, optimized, secure, and stable solutions—something that was not happening.

As a result, the overall satisfaction within the development teams remained low.

You may be saying - "this is a normal situation in many companies", "what is exactly the issue", may be the issue is "too many tasks or projects" ...

I would say Yes - this is considered "normal" in many companies, and I would say NO - this is not a normal situation in a company that wants to be successful.

The issue is not linked with the number of projects or tasks, even so, this part left uncontrolled may partially lead to such cases.

The same situation arose when I spoke with people. Many of them saw this as normal. In discussions about issues like incidents, prolonged delivery times, business dissatisfaction, or the lack of new technology adoption, the responses ranged from "we have no time for this now" to blaming others with "we can't deliver on time because something wasn't delivered to us," or "another department or team doesn't understand our challenges, which is why we have so many incidents." Another frequent complaint was about meetings; there were too many, preventing focus on work and leading to scattered efforts, directly impacting results.

Anyone reading this book can likely recall similar scenarios.

Now, let's examine what I did and the outcomes that followed.

My targets given by the CEO were to primarily focus on enhancing the engagement of technical teams, optimizing the implementation of Roadmap projects, minimizing incidents, and improving SLA stability.

Based on my previous experience, when addressing critical issues or starting new initiatives, I conducted a thorough assessment of the scope - to understand our current situation!

To gain a comprehensive understanding and to adopt a holistic perspective, I initiated a series of meetings with all stakeholders, both business and technical. To provide more detail:

- **With Technical Teams:** Engagements involved deep dives into their workflow, bug analysis, deployment frequency, architecture choices, tool utilization, and much more. Discussions were not limited to key technical personnel but included the entire team, either in group settings or through one-on-one meetings for critical case discussions.
- **With Business Stakeholders:** We explored their processes, gathered their expectations from the technical side, and understood their targets and the nuances of these goals.

Following several rounds of meetings and exchanges of information, I compiled a "Current Situation Analysis" as Point "A" and outlined the Targets as Point "B."

Then, the role of "navigator" began - charting the course from Point "A" to Point "B."

- If product quality was the issue, a dedicated workflow to enhance quality was established.
- If the challenge lay in project delivery, a follow-up process was initiated on one of the projects to closely examine the real-world functioning of the project process.

An action plan aimed at addressing the identified issues and enhancing the overall situation was then developed. This plan received consensus from both the team and business departments to commence implementation.

It's crucial to recognize that solving any issue requires a view of the entire process. Technical delivery improvements alone are insufficient without addressing the project requirements, testing, or launch strategy.

Here are the actions we initiated:

- **Focus on Product Quality:** This included enhancing product quality, addressing incidents, improving SLAs, adopting new technologies, and increasing team engagement:
    - **Incident Root Cause Analysis:** Key individuals prioritized understanding the root causes of incidents, dedicating time to discussions, log analysis, and action plans for testing in controlled environments. In the event of an incident, a collaborative effort was made to collect all necessary information for a thorough investigation.
    - **Proactive Technology Exploration:** Essential for staying abreast of new technologies, libraries, and versions. Each team leader designated an individual to spend half a day each week on R&D activities related to our technology stack. This was integrated into the regular schedule, with findings shared and assessed for applicability.
    - **Addressing Meeting Overload:** To mitigate the impact of excessive meetings, especially on longer tasks, a "no meetings day" was introduced, initially on a trial basis, later adopted permanently due to its effectiveness.

- **Roadmap Delivery Enhancements:** Improvements were made to both project and technical fix delivery processes to enhance efficiency:
  - **Unified Roadmap Creation:** A merged Business and Technical Roadmap provided a clear overview of project ownership, priorities, and resources, streamlining project management.
  - **Refined Project Initiation Rules:** Premature project starts were curbed by ensuring thorough initial specification analysis and clarity, leading to better resource allocation and minimized rework.

Guiding Principles for Action Planning were:
1. **Persistent Commitment to Quality:** Quality remains our paramount concern and is non-negotiable.
2. **Continuous Learning and Technological Advancement:** Keeping abreast of new technologies involves everyone in the organization.
3. **Unified Roadmap:** Projects are not divided into business and technical; all efforts towards product excellence are consolidated.
4. **Clarity Before Start:** Clear expectations ensure projects begin with well-defined objectives.

These approaches, part of our broader vision, values, and strategy, will be discussed in subsequent chapters.

The implementation of these processes was monitored over three months, emphasizing the importance of maintaining focus on key elements without being sidetracked by other priorities. This focus is a crucial aspect of IT leadership, necessitating collaboration with business stakeholders to underscore the importance of addressing critical issues promptly to ensure future work benefits from the solutions developed.

These were key results and takeaways (per domain):
1. **Quality Improvement:**
    - Systematic approach to addressing incidents, including architectural changes, and improved communication between technical and IT teams, resulted in a significant reduction in incidents after 3 months.
    - Implementation of additional metrics in the monitoring to detect warnings at an early stage helped prevent incidents.
    - Improvements in products and architecture were leveraged to enhance the quality of new products from launch.
2. **Peoples' Engagement:**
    - Encouraging continuous learning and the exploration of new technologies increased employee engagement and satisfaction.
    - Employees dedicated working time to learning, leading to heightened motivation as they witnessed personal and professional growth.
3. **Roadmap Delivery Enhancement:**
    - Initial challenges in roadmap delivery were overcome by changing the treatment of specifications, ensuring that work commenced only when requirements were fully specified and understood by both business and technical teams.
    - Iterative meetings and discussions resulted in a clear agreement on resource allocation, leading to more effective planning and reduced delays.
    - Improved specification clarity and

comprehensive answers to questions contributed to easier planning of resources and reducing the need for re-work, consequently enhancing product quality and therefore faster delivery.

An important aspect to highlight is that despite achieving the desired improvements, our efforts did not cease. Should we revert to previous work methodologies, the same issues would inevitably resurface.

In the subsequent period, we engaged in monthly reviews of our results, continually striving to enhance our work processes. The more improvements we implemented, the less stressful the work environment became, allowing team members to focus more on delivery and quality rather than on resolving recurring issues.

~~end of story~~

Constantly striving for efficiency is essential.

Efficiency underpins much of IT work, necessitating a mindset geared towards identifying and overcoming obstacles. This approach must become ingrained in our daily operations: it's not enough to merely be open to change - as CIOs, we must actively lead and drive it.

Without this proactive stance, much of the team's effort risks being wasted, akin to the scenario depicted in the accompanying image.

Picture 1: We are too busy ... to improve.

Let's begin now to delve into an overview of the roles and responsibilities of a CIO.

1.1 Assess Current Status

Understanding your present situation is similar to locating your GPS position. Neglecting to carefully evaluate where you stand today can lead to deviations in both strategy and implementation. For guidance in this critical assessment, the IT assessment template presented in **Chapter 2** (Table 1) can be a valuable tool.

The provided IT assessment template doesn't encompass every business sector. Specific sectors such as banking, healthcare, telecom, etc., may have unique requirements. These can be addressed either by listing them separately or by incorporating them into one or more existing domains or areas.

Employing IT assessment can act as a crucial initial step and a continuous benchmark, used regularly over time. For instance, conducting an internal assessment annually allows you to review these aspects, adding a column for the current date or the month and year, enabling a clear view of your IT's progression.

As your business and IT landscape grows, additional elements can be seamlessly integrated into the assessment.

1.2 Create Your Strategy

Crafting a strategy is not a one-time effort but an iterative process. By meticulously working on your strategy, you aim to reach from point A (the result of your assessment) to point B in X months/year (s).

I cannot emphasize enough how important it is to ensure that your strategy is clear! It has to be based on very simple principles, like the SMART (stands for Specific, Measurable, Achievable, Relevant, and Time-bound) principle and has to be transparently agreed upon with your business teams and the CEO.

Refer to the example of IT Strategy based on Business Strategy provided in **Chapter 3** (Building your Strategy).

> "PRODUCTIVITY IS MEANINGLESS UNLESS YOU KNOW WHAT YOUR GOAL IS."
>
> ELIYAHU M. GOLDRATT AND JEFF COX

1.3 Create And Manage Your Strategy Execution Roadmap

Once we have a Strategy (remember - it is point "B" where we want to be in a particular timeframe), it is necessary to build an execution plan! This plan should include tasks responsibilities for each domain and sub-domain, follow-up principles, and clear information about what means achieving the goal. The list of actions to execute the Strategy usually combines into a Roadmap. A well-defined roadmap facilitates breaking down complex tasks into manageable components. For reference, see the example IT Strategy Execution plan - Roadmap in the following chapters (Chapter 4)

Once a Strategy is established (envision this as point B, our desired destination within a specific timeframe), constructing an execution plan becomes imperative. This plan ought to delineate task responsibilities across each domain and sub-domain, outline follow-up principles, and clarify what constitutes goal achievement. The compilation of actions required to implement the Strategy typically takes the form of a Roadmap.

A meticulously crafted roadmap aids in decomposing complex tasks into manageable components. For an illustrative guide, refer to the example IT Strategy Execution plan - Roadmap provided in subsequent chapters (Chapter 4).

> "IDEAS ARE EASY. EXECUTION IS EVERYTHING."   JOHN DOERR

1.4 Manage Your Internal And External Processes

Why do I place such emphasis on processes? Many perceive processes as mundane, rule-laden procedures that suffocate innovation and creativity.

However, in my view, a process is far from being a "boring task." It is a mutually agreed-upon sequence of steps, communications, feedback, and tasks designed to achieve something beneficial for the company. Every occurrence in our lives and at our workplace is a process, whether explicitly defined or not. Thus, if we aim to allocate time and resources for innovation and fresh ideas, tasks that are similar in execution should be codified into a documented process. This ensures everyone knows their responsibilities, how to perform tasks, how to address issues, how to offer or process feedback, etc.

While it's unrealistic to expect processes to encompass 100% of work activities, effectively managing 80-90% through well-organized processes can significantly streamline operations and free up time for innovation and new ideas. It's crucial to simplify processes to eliminate unnecessary bureaucracy, making sure employees understand how to meet basic requirements efficiently. Below is an example of a simple process for equipping a new employee with basic tools:

"A new employee in need of a notebook and a pen is directed to a user handbook/FAQ. This resource outlines the necessary information and precise steps for requesting the required items for work and is available from their first day.

Such a streamlined process significantly reduces the time investment required from their supervisor or colleagues. Without such a process, each time the new employee needs something, they would need to inquire about procurement procedures, form submissions, approval processes, etc., from their superiors or peers. It's important to recognize that the absence of established processes can lead to frustration among new hires due to the constant need for clarification."

This example illustrates the critical importance of developing processes. Further details on processes vital for a CIO will be explored in the Chapters to follow (Chapter 5 and Chapter 9).

> "THE CIO PARADOX IS A SET OF CONTRADICTIONS THAT LIES AT THE CORE OF IT LEADERSHIP. THE PARADOX ENCAPSULATES THE DAILY CHALLENGES THAT CIOS FACE, AND IT IS WHAT MAKES THE ROLE SO DIFFICULT, AND SO INTERESTING."
>
> MARTHA HELLER

1.5 Build Your Team

Each Manager has a responsibility to properly manage the team which is entrusted to her or him.

Therefore, establishing effective management processes, from hiring to firing, is crucial for team leadership, motivation, and continuous growth. Building and managing the team is an ongoing responsibility—one of the most critical for a successful CIO.

We'll explore the subject of team management more thoroughly in **Chapter 6**.

1.6 Manage Technology

In today's business landscape, technology is integral to almost every industry. Properly managing technology is a primary responsibility of a CIO. If not managed effectively, technology can become a burden rather than a boon, causing more issues than benefits for the business.

This topic will be discussed in detail in Chapter 7.

1.7 Manage It Budget

The IT budget is an essential tool for organizations to allocate resources effectively, prioritize initiatives, and ensure that the IT department can meet the technological needs of the business. It is usually created in collaboration between IT management and the finance department, aligning IT expenditures with the overall strategic goals and financial constraints of the organization.

The importance of IT Budget planning and execution cannot be overstated - it is something which, if done properly, will enable the CIO and IT team to support business growth without restrictions.

A detailed view of the IT budget process and how-to will be discussed in Chapter 8.

You might wonder why these topics are so important for a CIO. Am I overlooking anything?

We can take a standard CIO Job Description and examine whether all the Key Responsibilities are covered (a practice implemented by Isabel Nyo, CTO and VP of Engineering, when describing the CTO role).

Using this approach, we can review a standard and common Job Description of a CIO and ask ourselves, "What have we covered?" and "Are we missing anything?"

CIO Job Description - **Key Responsibilities:**

1. **Strategic Planning:** Develop and implement a strategic IT plan that aligns with the organization's overall business strategy. Evaluate emerging technologies and assess their potential to enhance business efficiency and effectiveness.
2. **Leadership:** Provide leadership and direction to the IT department. Mentor and develop a high-performing

IT team to ensure the effective delivery of technology services and solutions.
3. **IT Governance:** Establish and oversee IT policies, procedures, and standards to ensure security, compliance, and efficient operations. Manage IT risks and ensure compliance with relevant laws and regulations.
4. **Budget Management:** Develop and manage the IT budget, ensuring cost-effective resource allocation and cost management.
5. **Project Management:** Oversee key IT projects, ensuring they are delivered on time, within scope, and on budget. Ensure effective change management processes are in place.
6. **Infrastructure Management:** Oversee the development, maintenance, and security of IT infrastructure, including hardware, software, and networks.
7. **Vendor Management:** Manage relationships with technology vendors and service providers, negotiating contracts and ensuring quality service delivery.
8. **Business Continuity:** Ensure robust disaster recovery and business continuity plans are in place and regularly tested.
9. **Innovation:** Foster a culture of innovation within the IT department, encouraging the exploration of new technologies and solutions to drive business growth and efficiency.
10. **Stakeholder Communication:** Act as a liaison between the IT department and other business units. Communicate IT plans, policies, and technology trends effectively across the organization.

We can observe from the list of responsibilities that all 10 requirements are covered in the chapters of this book. Some chapters address multiple elements simultaneously because they are interconnected.

Before delving into the specific responsibilities and challenges faced by CIOs, it's important to note that this book encompasses several fundamental aspects: a comprehensive list of responsibilities pertinent to CIOs, real-life stories from my experiences across diverse companies and sectors, and actionable advice for success and pitfalls to avoid.

You might wonder if a different management style from the author's would impact the usefulness of the advice and strategies in this book. While my leadership style may differ from yours, which is entirely normal, I choose not to detail various leadership styles, as opinions on their number and nature vary widely.

My leadership approach may adapt to factors such as "season", the company's current state, market conditions, and our objectives. However, responsibilities remain consistent, even though their importance may vary across different "seasons."

The key takeaway is that regardless of your leadership style, the practical advice and steps offered here remains relevant and applicable.

Outline of the Chapter 1: Your Journey as CIO

1. Assessing Current Status: Regularly conduct IT assessments to understand the current state and track IT evolution, adaptable across various business domains.

2. Strategy Creation and Execution: Develop and implement a clear, transparent IT strategy aligned with business objectives, including the creation of a detailed execution roadmap.

3. Process Management: View processes as essential tools to enhance efficiency and foster innovation, illustrated by the simple example of a new employee onboarding process.

4. Team, Technology, Budget: Direct your focus towards effectively building and managing these critical elements of your IT leadership responsibilities.

Your records: I encourage you to write down your conclusion/ ideas / actions from this Chapter. This action will ensure that the information you get will have practical utilization.

Chapter "Vs". My Vision and Values.

In the previous chapter, we examined the topics that will serve as the foundation for your role in IT leadership. Some may be less challenging, while others may present challenges. This variance depends on your prior professional experiences and your strengths or areas where you need improvement.

Before delving into the "puzzle" of the roles and responsibilities of a proficient CIO, I'd like to take a moment to encourage you to reflect on two fundamental questions: WHO AM I, and WHY AM I DOING THIS?

Why is this crucial? Drawing from personal experiences and extensive work with various managers and teams, a significant realization emerged - you can execute your tasks competently, yet find no satisfaction in your work, persistently wrestling with tasks or responsibilities. At times, you may question, "Why am I facing continuous challenges despite doing everything right?"

Hence, I urge you to redirect your focus: Who am I, and why are you doing what you do? Consider Your Vision and Your Values!

This isn't about creating something fancy or impressive, nor is it a slideshow to present to management and forget about. I'm emphasizing "your vision" - these two "Vs" should be uniquely yours.

Once you establish this Vision and these Values, they become the driving force that wakes you up in the morning, propelling you to push your capabilities to the limit, to persist in your work even when challenges are relentless.

And these two "Vs" should be aligned, like the well-known saying in the Bible: "A good tree cannot bear bad fruit, and a bad tree cannot bear good fruit." (Matthew 7:18).

To craft "My Vision & My Values," you need to pause, stepping away from routine work and thoughts about various issues and challenges. Reflect on what you want to become in 10 or 20 years, what you want to be remembered for, and the legacy you wish to leave behind.

I'm listing some reflection questions that may direct your thoughts to start creating your values and vision:

Q1: What can I do today, the result of which will be visible positively in 10-20 years?

Q2: How can I help my team become the best team we can be?

Q3: As a Leader, what I do to value my colleagues and their personalities as well as their efforts?

Q4: As an IT & Technology Leader, what I do to create a significant impact in the company I'm working in?

Q5: As an IT & Technology Leader and citizen, what I do to create a significant impact in society?

These "Vs" will serve as your foundation, upon which the "walls" listed and described in the following chapters will be built.

To help you build your values and visions, I'll share my "Vision & Values", as an example:

My Vision

- When working with every team, I value each person and contribute to her or his growth, fostering the development of the best team possible.

- In all my endeavors, I facilitate the growth, flourishing, and excellence of those around me.

- I am an integral part of my team, remaining connected through challenges, mistakes, and successes.

- I respect my manager/leader and strive to excel in the offered position and responsibilities.

- In IT, Technology, or Project Management domains (or any other domain), I aim to build optimal solutions, leveraging the team's potential each day, leaving no room for excuses.

- I actively promote the growth of individuals and work to maintain a positive team environment while actively removing toxicity.

My Values:

- I value truth and actively promote it.
- Honesty is a core value that I uphold and encourage.
- I value, provide, and accept support.
- Humility and kindness are esteemed values that I promote.
- Life, family, and health are significant values for me and others.
- Hard work is valued, and I strive to execute tasks professionally without excuses.
- I confront challenges confidently, knowing who I am.

I value these two "Vs" because, in my life and work, they have helped me avoid many troubles, prevented compromises with the truth, and allowed me to stay focused on good values. These Vs helped many of my colleagues in times of challenges and difficulties - when they were questioning if they were useful or not if what they do has any importance or not.

Hence, I encourage you to reflect on and start the development of your Values and Vision. Even if you choose not to undertake this exercise immediately and continue reading the book, consider revisiting this chapter later and preparing your "Vs."

A time will come when people question the difficulties, challenges, and struggles. Having your "Vs" will empower you to affirm: "We know who we are, and we know what we build, whatever the circumstances are!"

Your records: I encourage you to write down your conclusion/ ideas / actions from this Chapter. This action will ensure that the information you get will have practical utilization.

Chapter "C". Culture

In the previous chapter, we discussed some crucial elements - our Values and Vision. As mentioned before, they are fundamental to us both as leaders and individuals.

To progress on our journey to becoming successful managers and leaders, we need to build upon these foundations.

In this chapter, I want to delve into Culture: both Company Culture and IT Culture.

Since Values and Vision can vary among members of the management team, it's essential to have cohesive elements that act like glue for the management team and the entire company.

Following Values and Vision, the Culture within the company and your department or team is one of the most critical points.

Culture embodies the Values and Vision of the company and reflects how we act based on our Values and Vision.

Here is an example of the **Culture of the company**:

Openness and Honesty: In everything we do and say, we are committed to acting with complete openness and honesty.

Transparency: We ensure full transparency in every aspect of our work.

Proactiveness: We don't just wait for things to happen; we take initiative. We act proactively, not waiting for others to make the first move or to speak up. We lead with action and communication.

Trust: Mutual trust is the foundation of our team.

Unity: Despite our diverse roles and responsibilities, we are united as one team. We offer help, provide support through challenges, celebrate our successes and learn from our failures together.

Simplicity: Simplicity is at the heart of our client services. We handle the complexity of technology and processes internally, ensuring our clients experience ease and clarity.

Based on Company culture, and IT responsibilities, we need to have an IT internal culture sometimes called Manifesto.

It must be at the core of IT teamwork, in every aspect. You may take a lot of examples from the Internet, as many companies are sharing this kind of information.

I would propose one example here, an IT Culture (or Manifesto):

Quality and Excellence: uphold the highest standards of quality and excellence in every aspect of our work.

Adaptability and Resilience: we embrace change, learning from both successes and failures, and we are always ready to adapt to new challenges and opportunities.

Security and Privacy: recognizing the importance of security and privacy, we are uncompromising in our efforts to protect data and uphold the trust placed in us by our users and clients.

Client-Centric Solutions: we place the needs and experiences of our clients at the center of our design and decision-making processes. By understanding and anticipating their needs, we deliver solutions that not only meet but exceed expectations.

Innovation with Purpose: every technological advancement we pursue is aimed at improving efficiency, accessibility, and the quality of life for all.

Ethical Principles in Technology: we develop and implement technology with a keen awareness of its impact on individuals, societies, and the environment, ensuring that our contributions are beneficial and just.

Empowerment through learning: we are dedicated to

empowering individuals through education, providing accessible learning resources, and upskilling opportunities to ensure everyone can participate in and benefit from useful technology.

Teamwork, Respect, and Feedback: We recognize that our strength lies in each individual and the collective power of our team. We cultivate an environment of respect and mutual support, where every member is valued and empowered to contribute.

But these are not just words. A technology leader must be the promoter of this culture.

The Culture (or Manifesto) will ensure people know how to be a team, how to support each other, and how to act in many standard and non-standard cases.

Why does Culture or IT Manifesto matter?

For example, simple messages like "They don't understand me" can be changed to "I can support them, I can teach them to understand me or my work."

Instead of "I'm doing my work. They will do their work" we can change to "We are in the team. We are in the same boat. And when I finish my work, I help my teammates".

Doesn't matter. Is it IT or business? I can help them do their work properly with what I can.

Examples of such support:

A lot of times, the things, that matter and help for the team and organization to be efficient, are "in between the tasks" ... the tasks which are done by different people.

Meaning that a person finished the work. For example, created an API, and another person should test this API. The person who developed it can construct a bridge (documentation, an example of how to use it).

Now, these tasks are becoming easier because there are a lot of tools that are creating API documentation. And it is easier to do the API, to check the documentation if it is right or not. Test yourself, at least once or twice, to see that the API is functioning properly. And, finally, only after these steps to transfer the task to the QA engineer, for example.

The same can apply to the person who finishes an important task like "night work", like night planned maintenance. This person can write a short information/report:

- there was this change in the platform or the system.

- something was implemented.

- new software or update or patch was installed.

- how it was tested.

- what to do if something is not functioning well.

- who is the person who is replacing.

- the rollback procedure is this?

As we know clearly that Culture in the Company and within IT is important, I would like to dig deeper into two important approaches that are often either not done or not done properly: handover and feedback.

Culture of Handover.

A culture of handover ensures that every aspect of work within the company is documented, prepared for explanation, and shared with others.

In technology and IT, security measures like backups are

commonplace, where a copy of information is stored elsewhere. This ensures that if the primary information is lost or erroneously altered, we can recover it from the backup.

Another method of ensuring information security is load balancing, where both the primary and secondary copies of data are distributed across two or many systems. If one system fails, the other takes over without any loss of information.

I apply the same principle to managing people's responsibilities within IT teams.

This is referred to as the backup process, as well as the handover process: for all key positions and responsibilities within the IT Department or team, an IT leader should organize main and backup responsibilities.

For instance, if there are two systems, System A and System B, and two engineers, Alex, and Kent. Alex is more skilled in managing System A, while Kent is more adept at handling System B. Naturally, Alex will look after System A, and Kent will manage System B. This is often where the process ends for many teams...

However, an additional step is required: allocate some time for Alex and Kent to prepare instructions and assist each other in learning how to manage the system for which they are responsible. Once this is accomplished, implement a cross-backup for each other: when Alex is sick or on vacation, Kent will be responsible for supporting System A, and vice versa—when Kent is unavailable for any reason, Alex will take over the support for System B.

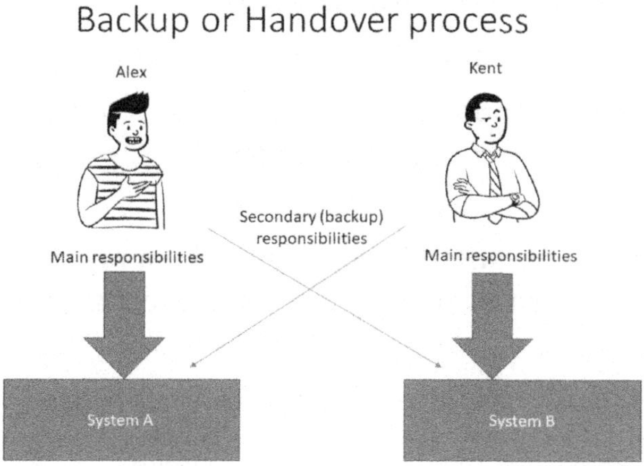

Backup or Handover process

Alex — Main responsibilities → System A
Kent — Main responsibilities → System B
Secondary (backup) responsibilities (cross-links)

Picture 2. Backup and Handover process.

In this approach, you guarantee that:

- There is a reliable backup of responsibilities and knowledge for critical systems and functions, ensuring continuity during vacations or illnesses.

- In the event of a departure, someone is ready to temporarily step in, especially for critical and support cases.

- A smooth handover process is achievable when someone leaves the company.

Typically, the backup person might not completely replace the primary responsible individual but can handle support cases, simple to intermediate configuration tasks, and maintain the system's operational health until the primary person returns or a replacement is hired.

To make this process effective, it's important for all IT personnel to:

- Document key tasks into instructions and share this knowledge with the team.

- Conduct handover sessions for significant system changes,

such as new versions, upgrades, or updates.

- Share critical system information on the Team's shared space.

- Encourage the secondary responsible person to participate in significant system work as part of a shadowing process.

As an IT leader, you should promote and oversee this process as a compulsory part of work for every critical area within the company.

Furthermore, it's crucial to apply this approach to your responsibilities. Identify team members who can advance in knowledge and responsibilities and invest in their development: openly share the core aspects of your work, the reasoning behind decisions, budget details, and issues with business and internal teams.

When you're away due to vacation or illness, avoid staying perpetually online (recall your "Vs" from the chapter on "Vs") - delegate your duties to one of these individuals. Rotate the delegation among different team members (based on the size of this group) each time you're away. This strategy ensures that the CEO, business teams and your teams know there are people within your team who are capable of taking on new challenges. It also motivates your team members to develop and grow.

Let's Summarize Handover and position Backup.

It is important to have a backup person for every key position in a department. This ensures that the work can continue uninterrupted in case of an emergency or absence. It is also important to have a process in place for handing over responsibilities when someone leaves the company. This helps to prevent a crisis and ensures that the company continues to run smoothly.

Culture of Feedback

I'm sure many of you aspire to work with a motivated team—a team eager to excel in efficiency, productivity, collaboration, innovation, and many other aspects that comprise a strong team.

You might wonder, how can I cultivate these characteristics within my team?

A crucial factor is effective communication within the team, primarily through feedback.

As a leader, you must practice and promote feedback.

This can be achieved through scheduled meetings: be it one-on-one sessions, team meetings, cross-team discussions, or meetings focused on a specific project, etc.

Yes, I understand, you're already swamped with countless meetings, discussions with business units, and an endless stream of emails and chats awaiting your response.

However, establishing a feedback culture should permeate all meetings, not just those set aside for feedback purposes.

Feedback, in our context, requires:

- Allowing everyone to express their thoughts on any matter.

- Feedback can be either positive or negative.

- Particularly with negative feedback, immediate reactions should be avoided. It might be beneficial to reflect on this feedback for a day, formulate some probing questions, and address these in a subsequent discussion.

To foster an environment where people feel comfortable offering feedback, consider the following approaches:

- Pose questions like "What is your opinion on this?", "What do you think we could do better, avoid altogether, or improve?"

- Inquire about personal performance - "What can I do to make your work more productive and satisfying?"

- During meetings about critical issues, ask "Why did this go wrong?" and "What can we do to resolve this quicker or prevent it from happening again?"

- When receiving feedback, it's often wise to document it and reflect upon it. Many times, we fail to notice issues within the team simply because we don't adequately consider the feedback given.

- Offer your perspective without initiating an argument: allowing some time between receiving negative feedback and discussing it can help diminish the impulse to argue. Typically, after expressing negative feedback, individuals are more receptive to exploring solutions together.

A culture of feedback is invaluable for bringing the team closer and enhancing efficiency, as it builds trust between team members and their leader.

Let's Summarize regarding Feedback:

Embed a feedback culture in every meeting and interaction. Encourage open, reflective dialogue on all feedback, fostering trust and innovation. This approach is essential for team growth and effectiveness.

Outline of Chapter "C". Culture.

1. Foundation of Values and Vision: Build Company Culture and IT Culture upon the foundational elements of values and vision.

2. Examples of Company and IT Culture: The importance of technology leaders actively promoting these cultures is evident in the examples of Company Culture and an IT Culture Manifesto.

3. The Importance of Handover and Feedback: Utilize both handover and feedback as practical elements of IT culture.

Your records: I encourage you to write down your conclusion/ ideas / actions from this Chapter. This action will ensure that the information you get will have practical utilization.

Chapter 2. Assessment of the status – AS IS.

As stated in previous chapters, the IT assessment is mandatory work when you either start your work as CIO, or you start a new season. A new season can be the beginning of the year, changing of business strategy, budget, or strategy preparation, or after some significant changes in the company (a big upgrade, a big launch, a big growth or failure).

This step should be initiated at the start of your assignment and can be repeated annually. This approach allows you to track progress, enhance your strategic approach, and address considerations related to efficiency, innovation, sustainability, speed, and security over time.

Real-life scenario: The absence of regular IT assessments leads to a crisis.

In a notable case, a Shadow IT system emerged within a company where the primary IT department held responsibility for core systems and oversaw various IT systems and applications across the organization. A specific business department opted to independently develop an in-house sales application, citing convenience and expedited delivery as primary motivations. They argued that internal development eliminated the need for extensive specification iterations and the prolonged wait times associated with IT deliveries.

However, consequences unfolded during a critical sales period when the IT department was urgently invited to a meeting with business directors. The discussion centered on significant problems attributed to the Sales application - numerous clients experienced service disruptions in stores, and sales targets were jeopardized. Understandably, blame was promptly directed at the IT department.

Upon thorough analysis, it became evident that the issues arose from the Sales application, developed internally by the Sales department. This application was not prepared for handling a substantial volume of transactions and lacked optimization for simultaneous use by multiple employees.

In response to the crisis, an immediate request was made for the IT department to rectify the situation by investing in additional equipment, albeit an unforeseen expense.

Eventually, a more strategic decision was taken to transfer the responsibility for the application to the IT department for ongoing support and maintenance. This transition not only facilitated the incorporation of necessary IT mechanisms for capacity management but also mitigated the risk of application failures during periods of high load.

Key takeaways from this story:

This scenario is that a comprehensive IT assessment can reveal functionalities and systems operating outside the scope of the IT department. This realization prompts discussions about implementing essential IT practices for all systems, particularly those integral to customer interaction - usually called Core Systems. By addressing these issues proactively, organizations can enhance their overall operational resilience and minimize risks associated with unmanaged IT systems, fostering a more robust and streamlined business environment.

~~ *end of story* ~~

How to do the IT assessment

Conduct a comprehensive assessment to understand "where we

are now" across various domains (see Table 1 below):

- Assess the state of the IT team.

- Evaluate the condition of the IT infrastructure.

- Examine the quality of IT services and adherence to SLAs for both internal and external clients.

- Review the handling of projects and changes as well as operational tasks requested by different departments such as "company/marketing/sales/etc..."

- Examine IT processes.

- Evaluate the current information security situation within IT.

Table1. IT assessment template (domains listed. some sub-domains listed as examples. You will need to list sub-domains depending on your organization)

#	Domain/area	Priority (set up priority based on your business type). Use 1-2-3 as priority matrix	Compliance (documented, process E2E (*end to end*), responsible for each domain, contracts available with clear responsibility matrix, etc. ...) Add Date (MM/YYYY)	Action - based on Compliance - action to improve, if any (this action should be part of the Change Management or Roadmap process)
1	IT organization and staff	1	if the domain is specific, you can list specific compliance requirements	
1.1	IT organization chart. Including number of employees, roles, titles, full or part-time status and local or remote location.		Example: IT structure – done, Team responsibility – done, Job descriptions for each position – done, all employees (internal and temporary included) - done	Example: If something is not done, add actionable item – complete "this" before "that" date
1.2	A description of IT departments/teams with purposes and responsibilities		Example: responsibilities of IT department, of each IT team	
1.3	Capacities, expertise - internal and external		Example: knowledge based on the systems available in the IT environment	
1.4	A list of vendors with proportion of IT expenses		Example: list of all IT vendors ordered by expenses	
2	IT infrastructure and Suppliers	1		
3	List of IT Software (CORE, Additional)	1		
4	Functional and SW architecture	1		

5	ITSM processes			
6	External partners			
7	Information security and Risks			
8	Project implementation processes, Business analysis			
9	Change Management processes, Business analysis			
10	SLA and Incident Management			
11	SW licenses			
12	Offices/affiliates			
13	Call center			
14	Data Warehouse and BI solutions			
15	Warehouse			
16	Testing			
17	Release management			
18	Documentation			
19	Current IT bottlenecks			
20	Current Reports			
21	Future projects driven by Business			
22	Future reports driven by IT			
23	Cost and Budgeting			
24	Software delivery, technical stack (front, back, etc...)			
N	Other domains depending on the functionality in the company (can be payments, data exchange between partners, security requirements, etc....)			

Approach this assessment with openness, clarity, and attention to detail.

While this exercise may initially require more time and temporarily divert the team from their routine tasks, its importance should not be underestimated. Thoroughly address each point, as it could prove to be a time-saving investment in the future and help identify potential weaknesses in your IT domain.

To conduct the IT assessment, collaboration with all stakeholders within the Business and IT teams is necessary.

Working with HR is crucial for analyzing IT staff competencies and knowledge, estimating training needs, hiring needs, or the necessity to outsource some functions to external companies or experts. Outsourcing may be necessary for short-term missions, especially if specific knowledge or experience is urgently required for a project.

It is also essential to collaborate with Customer Service, Sales, Marketing, and Finance to understand their challenges with the technology you oversee, their pain points and success stories, and complete the assessment with the necessary elements and actions.

Simultaneously, you and your team should evaluate each IT domain and sub-domain according to best practices.

Avoid "white zones" - areas that remain incomplete because they are not usually a priority. An example might be a task not initially planned by IT but emerged as a special requirement from the business: managing a company request mailbox where emails directed to different departments need to be forwarded to the respective department heads. If this task, deemed urgent, wasn't automated properly due to time constraints, and was instead handled manually by an engineer, it might become a permanent one, increasingly complex task for your IT team.

Such tasks should be reviewed and included in your plan to address all "white zones."

After engaging with all stakeholders and your internal team, the result will be a clear picture of your IT situation—a valuable starting point or re-evaluation marker.

If conducted properly, this assessment can prevent many potential issues for your company and customers.

Outline of Chapter 2: IT Assessment and its importance.

1. Evaluate Key IT Domains: Conduct thorough assessments of IT team, infrastructure, services, projects, processes, and security. Use a template to guide priorities and improvements.

2. Engage Stakeholders: Work with business and IT stakeholders, including HR, to understand challenges, identify training or outsourcing needs, and gather insights for the assessment.

3. Eliminate "White Zones": Ensure no area is overlooked by addressing unexpected or burdensome tasks, highlighting the need for automation and efficient planning.

4. Consider Strategic Outsourcing: Utilize outsourcing for specialized needs or short-term projects to enhance efficiency and focus on core competencies.

5. Develop an Action Plan: Use the assessment's insights to create a clear action plan, identifying improvement areas to prevent issues and enhance overall performance.

Your records:

I encourage you to write down your conclusion / ideas / actions from this Chapter. This action will ensure that the information you get will have practical utilization.

Chapter 3. Building Your Strategy

After completing the assessment and gaining a comprehensive understanding, our next focus point should be the IT Strategy - this is the point B on our map (point A is the result of IT assessment). In this chapter, we will explore the process of developing a sustainable IT Strategy that aligns effectively with your business goals.

Real-life case: building IT strategy.

A case from my experience: I led the IT team, and they were good, willing to learn and grow. However, what I observed was that each person was more focused on personal growth. While personal growth is not bad, when it becomes the sole focus, it can become detrimental to the company and the team.

Note: Your team will not be successful if people merely "do their tasks" and then "focus on their personal growth."

Learning from various management pieces of training, I realized that everyone wants to be part of something big, something more significant than just completing day-to-day tasks.

Even when I worked as an IT specialist, I realized... or better say, I expected a strategy for me and my team in line with something big - which is the company's strategy.

Therefore, I've requested from my supervisor what is the Strategy of our company and I've received the company's strategy goals. After meetings and discussions, I tried to understand the meaning of each bullet point of the strategy. Based on the business strategy, I started to build the IT strategy.

Initially, I thought about how to precisely align the business and

IT strategies because they are in different languages.

But if I don't try, it will remain unchanged — and that was not an option for me. Here are some examples of what I did and the logic behind it:

First example:

Business Strategy: Grow sustainable acquisition market share in volume and strongly improve our recently launched offers.

IT Strategy: "Implement and support Roadmap & Innovations: consider internal implementation (instead of supplier), consider cost, consider simplicity for the client!"

Result: IT should prioritize the Roadmap and Innovation, consider internal implementation, cost, and simplicity for clients in every product it builds.

Takeaways for this example: we built our work around this priority. IT people started working with business teams to understand simplicity, customer expectations, speed of functionality delivery without incurring additional costs, and how to improve product quality through enhanced testing and collaboration within IT teams and with the business.

Another example:

Business Strategy: "Improve the quality of services and differentiate ourselves through innovation."

IT Strategy: (Partially covered in the previous point) + this point is added: "Quality and Capacity: High Availability & Cost Efficiency – maintain preventive protection & implement agreed elements of the 'lean' program."

Result: The IT team focuses on properly managing the capacity of production systems and the quality of all services provided to customers. This involves understanding 'quality for the customer,' not just 'my system is working properly.'

This requires going beyond and talking to the business,

understanding their expectations and views on innovation, and helping the business use system functionalities for the company's benefit.

Takeaways from this example: For the team and each individual to grow, they need to see 'where we go.' By building the IT strategy based on the business strategy, we, as IT management, can help people be part of something big, allowing them to grow not just personally but also as part of the team. Their growth significantly improved team cooperation."

As a result of this exercise, we (me and my team) developed an IT strategy that was:

- aligned with the Business Strategy and was shared with the Business departments.

- aligned among different IT teams and known by each person in IT.

- easy to follow - easy to decompose into objectives for each team and each employee, thereby improving delivery, motivation, and engagement of each person in IT, and drastically enhancing cooperation between IT and Business.

~~ end of story ~~

Before we discuss the process of Strategy creation, an Important Note: A strategy may require adjustments or changes during its execution if the business direction, market demand, or regulatory rules shift. Therefore, it's crucial to assess the strategy regularly, which can be done on a monthly, quarterly, or half-yearly basis, depending on the scale of your company/project.

"PRODUCTIVITY IS MEANINGLESS UNLESS YOU KNOW WHAT YOUR GOAL IS."

ELIYAHU M. GOLDRATT AND JEFF COX

Here are the recommended steps to follow when you begin to develop your strategy.

3.1 Discover Business Strategy

Consult with the CEO/Founder

Approach your CEO to gain insights into the company's vision and strategy.

Engage with Business Teams

As you have the information from the CEO, you must work with other Business directors. Interact with your business team(s) to understand:

- Their strategy for the current year (and possibly for several years ahead).

- Practice patience, actively listen, take notes, and engage in discussions with both your team and theirs to align expectations.

To engage with business stakeholders effectively, start by creating a stakeholder matrix. Since IT and technology are utilized across all business units, maintaining clear communication, and understanding each unit's usage, knowledge, and expectations of IT and their tools is crucial. For some, technology usage might be as basic as starting a computer and accessing email, while for others, such as in Finance, tools like an ERP system are vital for daily operations, managing financial data, budgets, purchasing records, and more.

Here is a simple example of such a Stakeholder matrix.

Department	Responsible people	IT tools (core, non-core)	Expectations from IT	Information communication	Other

Sales	Director Responsible for Shops Responsible for Business customers	**Core:** Sales tool CRM ERP BI **Non-core:** Invoicing, Email Chat	Tool X should be available 24/7 Email is used to track clients' requests	Incidents, Maintenance preparation, New projects Or changes linked with Sales module, Shops infrastructure issue, etc.	

Based on your further needs, consider adding further details such as communication preferences, escalation paths and other useful information.

It's essential to maintain a table of this information, not strictly in document form but possibly within personal records or online tools. Having this table simplifies daily IT communications and understanding needs, facilitating interactions for any project or change.

Dive Deep into Capacity Planning

As the person in charge of technology, the CIO must ensure that all systems and applications align with business expectations concerning 'capacity,' which can encompass factors such as customers, documents, traffic, latency, and other key components integral to the technological solution:

- Emphasize the importance of delving deeper into capacity figures, understanding the type and quantity of clients expected in 1 year and beyond.

- Highlight the significance of IT being as expandable as possible to accommodate business growth.

- Anticipate scenarios where business projections exceed the initially planned capacity, ensuring that your IT infrastructure can scale seamlessly.

Ensure you maintain detailed data of all your systems, both production and non-production, including their capacity parameters. Record licensing details and hardware capacities—both maximum and recommended. Establish a "safety margin" for each parameter, which should vary based on the system, hardware type, or expandability speed.

This information is crucial for budgeting, monitoring, and planning purposes. Additionally, these metrics are vital for your backup and recovery strategy.

This information can be managed using a variety of tools, ranging from basic Excel or Sheets to more advanced ITSM (IT Service Management) or CMDB (Configuration Management Database) solutions such as iTop, Device42, ServiceNow, and others.

In summary, capacity planning is a critical aspect of IT management. As a CIO, it's imperative to manage this capacity effectively and communicate its importance to business teams for mutual understanding.

3.2 Build I T Strategy

- Develop an IT strategy based on the information received from the business teams and identify technological elements requiring improvements or transformation.

- Share the draft IT strategy with key team members and department managers, encouraging feedback and making necessary adjustments.

- Ensure the IT strategy becomes a dynamic, working document, not just a presentation for management.

- Remember your "Vs" (from Chapter "Vs") – and build the Strategy considering the above points and long-term Vision & Values.

3.3 Present Strategy To The Ceo And Business Departments

- Return to the CEO and business departments to present the IT strategy.

- Propose actions aligned with achieving their broader business strategy.

- Incorporate feedback and make required corrections.

As IT evolves, and technology progresses, IT management is no longer solely responsible just for the "technical infrastructure and staff". Technology has become an integral part of business more than ever. In this context, the person managing IT (Head of IT, CIO) becomes a part of the business.

By following these steps, you will have successfully crafted an IT/Technology strategy aligned with the business objectives for the designated timeframe, whether it's for the current year or the upcoming one, based on your preparation timeline.

In the Picture below you can see an alignment between Business and IT strategies:

(Example) Business strategy AND IT Strategy Hx 20xx

#	Action
1	Grow sustainable acquisition market share in volume and the strong improvement of our offers
2	Improve the usage of our "bundled products", cross-sell and upsell
3	Improve the quality of services and differentiate ourselves through innovation
4	Focus on simplicity of our offers, our communication and of customer experience, improve self-care
5	Continue efforts to improve career path of personnel, improve skills and boost engagement vis-a-vis the company
6	Maintain our costs at the level of "previous year" and control cash

4 pillars of IT for Hx 20xx

- Implement and support Roadmap/Innovations: consider internal implementation, consider cost, consider simplicity for the client!
- Quality and Capacity: High Availability & Cost Efficiency – keep preventive protection & implement "weak points removal" program
- Develop people, improve delegation, initiative taking and internal development
- Secured and Reliable IT network

Picture 3. Example of Business and IT strategy on one slide.

Outline of Chapter 3: Building IT Strategy

Consultation with Leadership: Initiate strategy development by aligning with the CEO/Founder's vision to ensure IT strategy complements the overall company strategy.

Collaborate with Business Units: Engage with different business teams to understand their strategies and objectives, facilitating a cohesive approach to IT planning.

Focus on Capacity Planning: Assess and plan for IT capacity to support business growth, anticipating future needs and scalability requirements.

Formulate the IT Strategy: Develop a comprehensive IT strategy that addresses insights gathered from business units, includes feedback from key stakeholders, and remains flexible for adjustments.

Presentation and Feedback Integration: Present the developed IT strategy to the CEO and business departments, incorporate their feedback, and refine the strategy to ensure alignment with business goals.

Your records: I encourage you to write down your conclusion / ideas / actions from this Chapter. This action will ensure that the information you get will have practical utilization.

Chapter 4. Create and Manage Your Strategy Execution Roadmap

In previous chapters, we've learned how to conduct an IT assessment and how to prepare our IT Strategy, meaning we have identified our current position ("Point A") and our desired outcome ("Point B").

Now, we need to construct a pathway from Point A to Point B.

This involves creating a detailed list of actions that can be monitored or implemented by IT teams and individuals. Maintaining a connection between each action and the overarching strategy is crucial.

Typically, this plan is developed in collaboration with your key personnel and/or managers. You'll review each aspect of the IT Strategy, identifying specific actions, projects, or tasks required to achieve the strategy's expected results.

It's also important to include estimated timelines, the anticipated impact on the business, and which departments will collaborate with or support IT in these efforts.

Remember your "Vs" from Chapter V, considering not only current challenges but long-term Vision & Values too.

Here is a sample of the IT Strategy Execution Roadmap.

IT Strategy: Actions plan Hx 20xx (1/2)

#	Action / project	Business impact + comments (if needed)	Timing	Refer to 6 major company priorities	Support/involvement of other departments
7	smooth preparation for next Hx 20xx roadmap - mid November – December		November-December 20XX	1, 2, 4	All departments
8	"weak points removal" program implementation	Partially done	H2	3	Technical
9	NEW TOOL pilot implementation	DONE	October-November 20XX	1, 2, 4	Technical
10	Dedicated trainings/activities for key people	Several training for PM is done and ongoing	Q4	5	HR
11	Get the experience with other companies, to learn "know-how" for different innovation projects		H2	5	Marketing, HR
12	Stabilize Reporting process – unify reporting KPIs	DONE partially. Implementation of all KPIs will be done in 20xx	Workshops with Business organized in August September. Final reports – November		Finance

IT Strategy: Actions plan Hx 20xx (2/2)

#	Action / project	Business impact + comments (if needed)	Timing	Refer to 6 major company priorities	Support/involvement of other departments
7	smooth preparation for next Hx 20xx roadmap - mid November – December		November-December 20XX	1, 2, 4	All departments
8	"weak points removal" program implementation	Partially done	H2	3	Technical
9	NEW TOOL pilot implementation	DONE	October-November 20XX	1, 2, 4	Technical
10	Dedicated trainings/activities for key people	Several training for PM is done and ongoing	Q4	5	HR
11	Get the experience with other companies, to learn "know-how" for different innovation projects		H2	5	Marketing, HR
12	Stabilize Reporting process – unify reporting KPIs	DONE partially. Implementation of all KPIs will be done in 20xx	Workshops with Business organized in August September. Final reports – November		Finance

Picture 4. Example IT Strategy Execution Roadmap on 2 slides.

Once you have created your Strategy Execution Roadmap, you need to do the following step: actions which are linked with 1 or more departments should then be part of Company Unified Roadmap.

When working on a Company Roadmap, consider the following key elements:

- Design the roadmap with a one-year perspective, detailing actions for the initial 3-6 months. For the latter part of the year, outline planned actions or projects, but remain flexible to adapt based on changes in priorities, budget allocations, or shifts in the business landscape.

- It's crucial to adopt an integrated approach that aligns the Business and IT/Technology roadmaps into a singular, unified company roadmap. This alignment helps avoid conflicts and ensures coordinated strategic planning. An example from Chapter 1 illustrates the significance of this integrated approach. The narrative highlights issues originating from having separate roadmaps, leading to conflicts. The resolution came through the development of a unified, integrated roadmap.

Having separate roadmaps often results in conflicts at various organizational levels, from CxOs to employees, leading to missed targets due to conflicting project priorities. To address this, ensure a single roadmap that provides:

1. Unified Project View: Present a consolidated perspective on both Business and IT/Technology projects.

2. Resource Allocation: Clearly outline how resources are allocated across projects.

3. Priority Visibility: Clearly communicate project priorities to all stakeholders.

4. Dependency Awareness: Provide a transparent view of project dependencies.

5. Cultural Alignment: Foster a culture of unity with the message that "we are all in the same boat."

Regularly review the Roadmap and Strategy Execution to maintain control and avoid resource gaps.

Consider the following meeting frequencies:

- **Monthly Basis:** Conduct meetings to discuss and agree on priorities, assess resource availability, and address risks and issues.

- Weekly Basis (IT/Technology Internal): Discuss project status, internal and client-related risks, resource dedication, brainstorm new ideas, and outline delivery scenarios.

- Weekly or Bi-weekly Basis (Business and IT/Technology Key People): Align teams working on ongoing projects, ensuring a synchronized approach.

For instance, in a project to launch a new service, the Technology team can provide delivery timelines, the Testing team can prepare for testing, the PR team can work on communication strategies, and the sales team can organize training sessions.

Decompose the roadmap into individual tasks and incorporate them into Individual Objectives and Key Results (OKRs), with a preference for a 6-month timeframe to ensure tangible results from both Business and Technology perspectives.

Outline of Chapter 4: Create and Manage Your IT Strategy Roadmap

1. **Develop an IT Strategy Execution Roadmap** that clearly outlines the steps from the current state to the desired future state, ensuring alignment with the Company and IT strategies.

2. **Incorporate IT initiatives into a unified Company Roadmap** to ensure coordinated planning across multiple departments, aligning IT efforts with overall business objectives.

3. **Plan with flexibility**, focusing on detailed actions for the next 3-6 months while allowing room for adjustments in the roadmap for the latter half of the year.

4. **Adopt a unified roadmap approach** to prevent conflicts between business and IT/Technology plans, promoting a culture of collaboration.

5. **Regularly review and adjust the roadmap**, employing

monthly and weekly meetings to keep the execution aligned with strategic goals and adapt to changes efficiently.

Your records: I encourage you to write down your conclusion / ideas / actions from this Chapter. This action will ensure that the information you get will have practical utilization.

Chapter 5. Management of Your Internal and External Processes

In previous chapters, we've learned how to identify the current status and how to build the roadmap to the destination.

To reach the destination, plans alone are not enough - you need tools, signs, resources, means to do the work, and people to work with.

What is a process? It is a series of actions or steps taken to achieve a particular end. In a business or organizational context, a process refers to a set of interconnected activities or tasks that, when performed in sequence, aim to accomplish a specific goal or objective.

This is exactly what we need to build to reach the expected or planned result.

In this chapter, we begin to discuss processes - the means and tools that will help you and your teams realize the roadmap.

As the individual overseeing Technology and Information, the Chief Information Officer (CIO) plays a pivotal role in orchestrating various processes. While not exhaustive, the following processes are essential.

5.1 Service Level Agreements (Slas)

SLAs with Suppliers:

Establish clear agreements compliant with Business and Regulatory requirements for hardware, software, and IT services. Direct collaboration with the Business is crucial to dispel misconceptions about IT capabilities and limitations.

If these requirements do not already exist, they must be developed in collaboration with the business. It is crucial to avoid perceiving IT/Technology as either having 100% availability or being obligated to accept any change request instantly due to Agile practices. The capacity of systems should not be assumed to be unlimited simply because auto-scalability is enabled; there are still limits even in such environments.

As a result, one of the roles of the CIO is to guide business colleagues on how to perceive IT/Technology. This involves understanding its functionality, usage parameters, limitations, and the correlation between SLA percentages and capacity/licenses/budget.

External SLA is important!

Whether you are providing services with an SLA, or acquiring services with an SLA, it is a permanent part of any service. Within this wording, there is the term "agreement" which means - we agree to provide OR use the services with this service level.

Real-life story regarding the importance of external SLA.

My team and I were responsible for a platform, serving

customers real-time services.

The SLA for such a platform is 24/7 and it is quite costly. Sometimes, over time, an SLA can cost you more than the platform itself.

But let's come back to the story.

That Saturday, I was called by the Supervision team - "services are down completely." Even though the platform was secured with all necessary (at that time) measures, it was completely down.

A colleague picked me up from home, and we drove to the office and data center.

At this stage of my work, I had all the necessary training, knew how to operate, and could do almost anything with this platform and the OS and the DB inside. But I was not prepared for a crisis - and I started to enter into a panic mode.

Most probably many of you remember this feeling... you open a terminal and think - "what am I going to do right now?" (for me it was the first incident of such scale and with this platform).

Moreover, many people, directors, managers, teams were waiting for when the problem will be solved. It is Saturday morning, and people are not able to use our services.

At this stage, you understand how important the SLA is!!!

I opened the document, found the phone number and email of the 24/7 support team, and called them.

In the meantime, I collected information from logs thinking: "why the platform is down while OS and DB and Application Software are up and running?" (fast forward - here I was wrong because the issue was with the DB, not running properly).

I called and explained - "we are this and this company, we have this issue". They asked for access - a process which was exactly part of the mentioned SLA. They connected, tried many things which didn't really help.

I was cooperating with them, proposing some actions, trying together with them, didn't help either.

While trying to solve it, I realized that the pressure is not as intense when you work with the team to find a solution! The panic disappears!

The impact was already about 4 hours - which was a very critical threshold for our company!

My director asked for details and kept me separated from other teams... so that I could be focused on the solution.

(Note) it is very and very important for IT management - when you have an incident, to let your team DO the work focused on the solution, protect them from external questions, and handle the internal communication on your own.

When services are disrupted, the impact on the entire company is substantial.

Retail outlets face operational challenges, as customers, unable to access services, turn to nearby stores for information. These shops, also serving as service centers, are expected to provide updates on incidents and estimated resolution times.

Customer Service was inundated with inquiries, with customers eager to know when services would be restored. The surge in call volume was so significant that the department had to call in extra staff to manage the overwhelming demand.

From a technical standpoint, if one system fails, others may become overburdened due to a spike in customer activity. Consequently, technical teams must prioritize the maintenance of systems under their purview to ensure continuity and prevent further disruptions.

But let's come back to the incident and what was next.

The remote support team called their experts to be involved because everything they tried was not solving the issue. Finally, I got on the phone with their database expert, and we started to analyze what is happening with the database... and found out that there was a broken index that didn't react to the command to recover.

It was the first breath of fresh air - apparently, we found the reason. Now we need to solve it. The database expert explained I needed to get all the services down, put the database in single admin mode, and try one more time to recover this index. This operation could be done only by me because it will restrict all the outside communication.

There were already more than 5 hours of services unavailable.

I did the recover command... and it worked! The database check passed successfully, and I started to run the services one by one.

The impact was almost 6 hours! Services recovered, customers started to use the services, we were up and running!

The Takeaway from this story:

Basically, I knew all the actions that were done by the support engineers and their database expert. But in such a crisis, you need a team that can work under pressure, guide you to follow a process, or give them access to do it. You need a team that will confidently, step by step, recover the services.

And for these people and these teams to operate properly, and for services to work properly - you need an Agreement, a Service Level Agreement.

~~ end of story ~~

Next SLA is **the SLAs for Internal Clients.**

Clearly define responsibilities, escalation paths, response times, and communication channels for employees seeking IT/

Technology support.

When you, as an employee, have a request that needs to be addressed by the IT/Technology team, you should:

1. Clearly understand who is responsible for handling the request.

2. Be aware of the appropriate channels and individuals to contact when making a request.

3. Have a realistic expectation of the time required to fulfill the request.

4. Know the proper escalation path in case the request is unresolved, or the outcome is unsatisfactory.

5. Be informed about the designated application or communication method to use when submitting the request (which can include email or chat).

Real-life story - Implementation of Internal SLA.

I'd like to share a real-life story about when we implemented an Internal SLA and the outcomes we achieved.

Globally, the company was performing well, acquiring customers, selling, and providing quality services.

The service quality was good to excellent, and all teams were functioning properly.

However (there is always a 'but')... there were instances when my CEO would call me and inquire why something wasn't working, why customers were dissatisfied, or why there was an incident he was unaware of.

I had to understand the exact issue. After clarification, it became apparent that one of our customers was not activated properly, unable to use our services, leading to their complaints - which translates to 'our services are not working'!

Upon delving deeper, I realized that there were cases where we spoke 'different languages' and perceived services or products differently.

For instance:

- A technical person verifies that systems are working properly, concluding that services are under control.

- The CEO or another businessperson receives a call from a VIP customer complaining about the inability to use our service, interpreting it as a flaw in our services.

We had many cases like this, which didn't improve the working atmosphere. We faced constant pressure and occasional conflicts between teams and departments. Many of you may have experienced this: pressure from management, misalignment between technical and business aspects, miscommunication, etc.

However, with our primary goal being the success of our company and a positive customer experience, we realized the need to come together and:

- Align our understanding of the quality of our service/product.

- Align our understanding of incidents.

- Align our understanding of customer and mass issues.

- Clearly define roles and responsibilities.

- Agree on a process for solving each case with quality, the right tone of voice, and promptly.

- Perform our work with the 'customer in the room'.

Combining all the above, we started building a process called: Internal SLA and Incidents Management.

For this purpose, we discussed, agreed, and included in the document:

- Defined all types of issues and KPIs - all aligned between different teams.

- Clarified responsibilities.

- Specified actions for each team when 'this' happen.

- Designated technical/IT responsibilities per domain.

- Outlined how we handle cases: incidents, mass issues (more than X customers), unique customer issues, issues of VIP customers, etc.

- Set timing requirements/necessities for answers or solutions.

- Established an escalation matrix in case the issue/incident is not resolved in time or not resolved properly.

- All done with 'clients in the room'.

As a result:

- We increased our understanding of quality for the client.

- Implemented measures that improved customer experience (such as additional checks after human work and additional tests).

- Enhanced the quality of our products and services.

- Improved internal cooperation - no more ping-pong messages during incidents or issues.

Takeaway from this case:

Even if each team was doing its job properly, we realized that as a company, we were perceived in a fragmented way. Focusing on overall quality and putting the company first in our work through the implementation of this 'Internal SLA' process not only improved the quality and perception of our company but also strengthened our internal cooperation, making us a more cohesive team!

~~ end of story ~~

SLAs for External Clients.

Tailor service quality, availability, responsiveness, and complaint resolution based on regulatory requirements or business needs.

In certain business sectors, these requirements may originate from regulatory bodies within the country where your operations are based.

In the absence of regulatory bodies, such requirements must be established by business teams with the assistance of legal support.

For example, an e-shop website must adhere to the following criteria:

1. Ensure a responsive system, especially during high-traffic periods such as Black Friday or the holiday season, to prevent customer wait times.

2. Maintain real-time synchronization of available stock with purchased items.

3. Provide a 24/7 online payment option.

4. Implement robust security measures to eliminate any risks of compromising personal data.

5. Ensure that all processes, from the moment a customer pays until the goods are received, operate smoothly, accompanied by appropriate notifications, warranties, and so forth.

Technical SLA

Internal technical SLAs apply to all Datacenter elements, encompassing power, conditioning, and other related components.

5.2 Information Security

The Information Security process includes, but is not limited to, the following:

- Providing training for newcomers.

- Implementing all necessary security rules based on information categorization.

- Maintaining strict access rules integrated with the hiring and firing. Upon hiring a new person, an access request should be initiated based on the employee's responsibilities. When an individual leaves the company or takes a long-term leave (e.g., sickness, pregnancy), there should be an immediate suspension or closure of access for that specific person.

How to Start Building an Information Security Program: Begin with Simple Steps.

NOTE: I am not presenting any technical tools here because it all depends on the technologies your company uses. I aim to provide examples of processes, based on my experience and the current trends in various companies I have worked for or learned from.

1. Define Information Categorization and access rules for your company, if not yet defined. This means creating a simple document (later can be detailed) with a table where you list the information you possess and its level of confidentiality for you and your clients. Below, you can see an example of such a table.

Type of Information	Sensitivity Level	Description	Who Has Access (Role)	Who Has Access (Department)
Employee Personal Information	Confidential	Details about employees, including contact information, social security numbers, and personal details.	HR Managers, Department Heads	Human Resources
Client Financial	Secret	Financial records	Account Managers,	Finance, Account

Information		and transactions of clients, including account numbers and investment details.	Finance Team	Management
Internal Project Plans	Internal	Plans and documents related to ongoing and upcoming internal projects.	Project Team Members	Relevant Project Departments
Strategic Business Plans	Secret	High-level strategy documents outlining the company's future direction, goals, and initiatives.	C-Level Executives	Executive Management, Strategy
Operational Procedures	Internal	Documents detailing the standard operating procedures, workflows, and guidelines for company operations.	All Employees (as required)	All Departments
Marketing Strategies	Confidential	Plans and analyses related to marketing campaigns, target markets, and product launches.	Marketing Team, Strategic Planners	Marketing, Strategy
Research and Development Data	Secret	Information on new technologies, products in development, research findings, and innovation strategies.	R&D Team, Selected Executives	Research and Development
Financial Reports	Confidential	Reports containing detailed financial performance, forecasts, and budgets.	Finance Team, C-Level Executives	Finance, Executive Management
Legal Documents	Secret	Contracts, agreements, and other legal documents that could affect the company's operations and rights.	Legal Team, C-Level Executives	Legal, Executive Management
IT System Credentials	Secret	Usernames, passwords, and other credentials necessary for accessing company IT systems.	IT Administrators, Security Team	Information Technology

Table 2. Example of Information Categorization.

Where Sensitivity Level is:

- **Secret** is the highest level of sensitivity, used for information whose unauthorized disclosure could cause serious harm to the company or its clients.

- **Confidential** is used for information that, if disclosed without authorization, could cause harm or damage.

- **Internal** is used for information that is not public but is less sensitive than Confidential information; unauthorized disclosure is undesirable but not expected to cause serious harm.

This table serves as a valuable tool for managing information security and ensuring that sensitive data is appropriately protected.

2. Build Basic Information Security Rules for the Company Based on These Concepts: Confidentiality, Integrity, and Availability.

These can be key topics presented to each new employee, among others:

- Passwords for accounts - establish rules for password creation and complexity necessary to prevent guessing.

- Email usage - guidelines on how to handle emails from unknown senders or unexpected emails with attachments, even from known contacts.

- Prohibit running unauthorized software.

- Prohibit sharing access credentials with others.

3. Develop Necessary Information Security Policies (note: this is not an exhaustive list):

- Password policy - from day one, implement password rules, especially for management accounts and IT experts, though not exclusively.

Even though there is a trend towards passwordless access, passwords will continue to be used for many systems for many years to come.

- Access policy - based on Information Categorization, construct necessary groups and user accesses that will be strictly required to complete tasks for a specific team, function, or individual.

- Backup policy - a policy to back up all necessary data, detailing how to do it, how often, and where to store the backups. Remember to consider regulations like GDPR (General Data Protection Regulation, EU Regulation), which restrict how long certain information can be stored in backups or archives.

- Encryption policy - guidelines for securing information within systems, particularly databases.

In this subsection, I've outlined basic steps to ensure your company's Information Security receives adequate attention. Given the current environment, these actions and steps may not suffice, and you may need to collaborate with Security Teams to develop more sophisticated solutions, utilizing SIEM solutions, penetration testing services, bug bounty programs, and others. Discussing these areas in detail is beyond the scope of this book, but you can consult specialized books and articles on Security for more information.

5.3 Change Management Process

The Change Management process must be clear and transparent, providing solutions for various changes. In some cases, the solution may involve addressing the issue in the next sprint or project, while in others, it might entail a decision by the Budget Committee to assess the eligibility of a change that incurs costs, such as system replacement.

This process should encompass IT domains, designate responsible individuals for each domain, establish clear timelines, and include an escalation matrix.

Furthermore, the Change Management process needs to be interconnected with the Roadmap process, serving as one of the entry points (especially when a required change becomes part of a project). Additionally, it should align with internal SLAs, particularly when an issue or incident necessitates a change implementation.

real-life case - failure to have a consistent long-term approach to the needed changes.

Throughout my more than two decades as a CIO, one notable lesson stands out— the significance of laying a solid foundation for processes, particularly when it comes to the Change Management and Roadmap. The impact of a lengthy and unstable Roadmap process on business requirements cannot be overstated.

As the company experienced rapid growth, the demand for numerous applications to keep pace with customer acquisition intensified. However, the Roadmap process in place proved far from ideal. The perpetual shifting of requirements from various business departments to the bottom of the priority list resulted in constant delays in implementation.

Unsurprisingly, the consequences of an unstable Roadmap were felt deeply. Most IT resources found themselves absorbed in marketing projects due to frequently changing priorities. Projects from other departments languished with lower priority, occasionally getting deferred from one year to another.

In response to these challenges, a visionary departmental head took matters into their own hands. Faced with the impact of lower-priority projects on customer service, they initiated the formation of a dedicated IT team within their department. This team set out to develop applications that streamlined the handling of customer documents and requests across different teams.

Initially, these applications proved highly effective, allowing the department to manage its workload adequately. However, as customer numbers surged, the limitations of the disparate systems became increasingly evident. During peak customer activity periods, processing delays became pronounced, posing a significant risk of losing valuable customers to competitors.

Imagine the following situation: there is a major promotion during the holiday season. Many customers hurry to take advantage of the new offer, willing to queue just to secure a great deal for themselves, their families, or even part of their staff.

They wait in line, complete the paperwork, pay for the service, and... they expect the offer to be activated as soon as they leave the store. But - the services are not available. They call after 1 hour - no result, call again in 3 hours - still no result. You can truly understand the frustration when you've done everything required, but the company fails to deliver the promised services.

Meanwhile, inside the company's customer service department, the scene is chaotic: the staff is overwhelmed, extremely busy, and exhausted. Each employee must navigate between 3-4 different interfaces, extracting information from one interface to input into another, then activating something in a third interface, and then... updating information in the first two interfaces again. With such a process, mistakes are inevitable, stress is guaranteed, and delays are a direct consequence of such stressful manual work.

The root of the problem lies in the lack of integration among several systems and applications. Requests flowed through two separate systems, with subsequent processing scattered across various platforms, each requiring manual intervention.

Upon addressing this issue, we launched an integration project. Systems were equipped with APIs to process different request types, ensuring synchronization of all client requests across platforms. The integration not only streamlined the request process but also automated controls and status updates.

Key Takeaways from this story:

1. Integration for Seamless Operations: systems handling client data must be integrated to minimize manual work, enhance control over execution, and bolster security and access to customer data.

2. Early Adoption of Roadmap Process: the roadmap process should be instated in the early stages of the company's growth, allowing for clear prioritization and strategic planning.

3. Prioritization with Long-Term Impact in Mind: when establishing priorities, consider the long-term impact on the company's brand and positioning within the market matrix. Prioritization shouldn't just be about immediate needs but also about sustaining and elevating the company's standing over time.

~~ end of story ~~

5.4 Roadmap Process And Related Elements

In order that Roadmap process is functioning properly, several elements must be in place for each company. If they are not in place, the CIO should drive this change and propose to implement such processes.

Here are some elements which are key for an efficient Roadmap process:

- **Understanding Project Management Methodologies**: Familiarize teams with project management methodologies to enhance project execution and avoid misunderstandings. Details on the PM methodologies are described in Chapter IX.

- **Components of Roadmap:**

    - **Projects**: Clearly prioritize projects aligned with Strategy Execution.

    - **Events**: Plan for special events requiring preparation and presentation.

    - **Improvements**: Include refactoring, infrastructure changes, and non-client visible modifications.

    - **Changes**: Address change requirements with a clear decision-making process.

- **Programs, Portfolio, Projects:** Align all initiatives within a **Unified roadmap**.

- **Role of Project Management Office (PMO):** PMO should report to the CEO, and all the departments, including Technology / IT, should align with the type of PMO defined by the company, with necessary internal flows/processes, and established reporting structures.

Here, I want to emphasize an important aspect: the PMO should report directly to the CEO. Why is this significant?

All ideas originating from different departments need to be evaluated, prioritized, and approved at the company level. If the PMO is part of any department (not reporting directly to the CEO) and reports to its director, then the evaluation and prioritization process might not fully consider the benefits for the company as a whole but rather focus on the benefits for that specific department.

When the PMO reports to the CEO, the leader of this team can challenge any department's ideas and present them to the CEO for arbitration. The outcome of such a process will be significantly more beneficial for the company!

---

real-life case of how a Roadmap process was created and managed.

After the launch of the company and launch on the market, we had several months of "solving the issues," which involved addressing all the problems resulting from a fast and full launch. It took about six months to resolve them all.

Then we created and initiated the Roadmap process in order to ensure proper delivery of Projects for the benefit of the company.

The process by itself was simple (don't hear "easy" please), but without following the right process, it did not work properly.

There was a dedicated PMO person responsible for collecting all the ideas, project information, and statuses.

PMO reported directly to the CEO of the company - this was one of the CRUCIAL points. The roadmap was unique for the Company, including projects from all departments!

The Roadmap process was divided into two parts:

- **Preparation of the Roadmap**.
- **Roadmap delivery**.

Below, I'll describe both processes and the result.

Preparing the Roadmap.

Roadmap was divided into Half-Year Roadmap(s) and this is how it was filled with ideas/projects.

- Three months before the start of the next half-year (beg October for H1 next year), each department should provide its list of projects with additional details:
  - Concept of the project
  - Reason for the project - what exactly this project is going to bring to the company/department.
- The IT department also provided a list of technical projects planned for the next period, including migrations, new equipment implementation, upgrades, new versions implementation, among others.
- During the next month, IT needed to analyze all concept documents and provide initial The feedback from IT included complexity (easy, moderate, complex), duration, dependencies, and any key risks.
- After feedback from IT (and other departments) was analyzed and discussed in several meetings, prioritization was introduced, some projects were removed, and resources were discussed and agreed (financial, teams, people, suppliers).
- At the end of November, the Roadmap for H1 was ready and approved, and planning started.
- As projects were validated by the end of November, during December detailed specifications were under preparation - they had to cover at least 3 months of the

next Roadmap delivery period.

The same exercise started at the beginning of April for H2.

- With the same sequence of actions, the final approved roadmap for H2 was ready at the end of May.
- (Similar to the explanation above) During June, detailed specifications for the first three months were under preparation and discussion.

As a result of Roadmap preparation:

- All teams knew which projects had to be implemented in the following Roadmap period.

- For each project, there was a confidentiality policy, and responsible people were dedicated from each department.

- (Note) The Roadmap covered 80% of the time of people responsible for development and implementation. Why? Because we needed to keep a 20% safety margin for fast projects, reactions to competition, and fast changes linked with some specific events that were unknown in advance.

Roadmap Delivery

Since Roadmap creation was clear, and we had the Roadmap "file" (you can use any tool here, from Excel / Sheets to Jira or any other) updated and clear for all, it was necessary to organize the Roadmap delivery process properly.

Before going into the details of delivery, several key elements of the Roadmap delivery process:

- It doesn't matter if you deliver projects in a waterfall or agile manner - they all have a start time, launch time, status, risks, allocated resources, and priority. Therefore, the status of the project was important at each stage (details about PM methodology you can read

in Chapter 9).
- Simultaneous projects - it was agreed that there are a maximum of five simultaneous projects in the active phase of development, implementation, and testing at the same It was linked to three elements:
  - Availability of five people inside IT who were responsible for project delivery.
  - Availability of businesspeople to write and rework the specifications and clarify all the details with other departments.
  - Availability of other teams: testing, marketing, etc.

Note - The simultaneous number of projects is a crucial element of the Roadmap delivery process. It should not be too small, as people will be working lightly, and it should not be more than the capacity, as people will not be able to control more details and will not be efficient enough to have a good delivery flow.

- Inside the IT department, there were five people responsible for the project - they were called SPOC (Single Point of Contact). When the project was initiated, one of these people was allocated to the project based on internal discussions we had. This element of SPOC was crucial - this is why: inside each project, there were different IT teams responsible for their subsystems. SPOC was responsible for clarifying, challenging, and proposing solutions for internal IT teams for their project so that the solution would be optimal in terms of cost, and time, and Businesspeople responsible for their projects mainly worked with IT SPOCs. For one project: without SPOC - the project duration could be 7-8 weeks; with SPOC - the project duration was 3-4 weeks.

Now, as key details are known, I'll describe how the Roadmap delivery worked:

Each week there was a Roadmap status meeting.
- The main scope was:
    - Discussion about five simultaneous projects.
    - Removing risks or barriers.
    - Clarifying priorities in case of new elements, ideas, or projects.
    - Reprioritization in case a new project was included in the Roadmap.
    - preparation for coming projects - readiness of specs, experts, budget.
- People involved:
    - Businesspeople responsible for their budget.
    - CEO of the company.
    - PMO or main PM
    - Main directors or their deputies participate in the delivery.
    - CIO
    - IT SPOC people responsible for delivery.
- Before this Company Roadmap status meeting, inside IT, we had our internal Roadmap status meeting:
    - We had to prepare the statuses.
    - We had to prepare the information about risks.
    - We had to inform/propose solutions and discuss issues.
- Before the launch of the project, there was a specific meeting, "pre-launch Project X meeting," where all the responsible people had to participate. During this meeting, all the teams were aligned based on a Checklist. In such a way, no delivery was approved if a small but critical detail was missing or not done properly.

Having these two processes, we were ensuring:

- The Roadmap was consistent with the needs of the business.

- The Roadmap was under total control.

- Before the launch, all the projects/products were verified very carefully.

Takeaway from this story:

The process we built was not complex. It was simple and based on agreements between all the departments.

All the statements above helped the company be successful in delivering a very big number of projects. Such a performance was almost impossible for our competitors.

~~ end of story ~~

5.5 Tools For Roadmap And Task Management

- Utilize tools such as Excel/Sheets, PowerPoint/Docs/Slides, Jira, Trello, Zoho, ClickUp, Confluence (for task management if Jira is used), and Microsoft Project for more extensive projects.
- Don't focus on tools but focus on proper If the process is acceptable, and covers all elements E2E (end to end), then you can use the right tool. The tool itself will not solve a broken process.

real-life case - the implementation of a roadmap/task management tool significantly improved the organization of operational and project work within a team.

While working at a company, I was appointed as the manager of a new team. Though not large, the team's responsibilities spanned various areas: we were tasked with development, project participation, and supporting certain non-production systems.

The diversity of our responsibilities made it challenging to track which tasks were planned, which had been completed, and what remained for any given project or task.

To better coordinate our tasks and manage our resources, we found it necessary to hold separate meetings to discuss statuses, address issues, and plan how to tackle the remaining work.

Although we reached a consensus on our synchronization process, the varied nature of our tasks made us realize the need for a tool to share this information effectively, as emails and chats were insufficient.

At that time, the company lacked a specific tool to meet our needs.

We decided to implement Jira, choosing it for its simplicity and our prior experience with it. I'm not endorsing this tool; there are many similar options available.

We created user accounts for all team members and began organizing our work within the tool.

Setting up was straightforward. We decided on a Kanban board with several sections:

- TODO: All tasks assigned by person and project, including necessary priorities and deadlines.

- IN PROCESS: Tasks currently being executed.

- IN TEST / UNDER REVIEW: Tasks requiring testing or peer review.

- DONE: Completed tasks.

The process was simple:

- Based on priority and criticality, the responsible person would take a task from the TO DO section (backlog), move it to IN PROCESS, and begin work.

- Movement to other sections depended on the task's status.

- The responsible individual was required to document all relevant details within the task: input documents, steps taken, and other task-related information.

As a result:

- We efficiently organized our project and operational work.

- We eliminated the need to inquire about statuses or availability for tasks and meetings.

- We achieved clarity in terms of timing and actions for each task.

This experience highlights the ease and effectiveness of using a straightforward tool to organize tasks and operational processes, significantly improving team workflow.

~~ end of story ~~

5.6 Monitoring And Support Processes

- Implement robust Incident Management processes, possibly incorporating Problem Management for a comprehensive approach.

Real-Life Story: Enhancing Monitoring and Support Processes

This narrative shed light on practical steps to enhance the monitoring and support processes within an organization.

Following the implementation of all production systems, monitoring tools began aggregating various issues, including warnings and alarms. While IT experts could easily decipher these alerts, understanding their implications and identifying the components at risk, the scenario was different for the monitoring and support teams. These teams, tasked with overseeing a broader range of systems beyond IT (such as security systems, specialized applications for retail, customer service, etc.), found each IT-generated alarm to be a novel challenge.

The process for addressing each alarm or warning typically involved contacting a designated IT specialist or even the CIO. However, due to the unclear nature of the alarms, misdirected calls were common, leading to frustration among team members who were roused at inconvenient hours for issues outside their responsibilities. This not only affected service and solution delivery times but also reduced team morale.

Furthermore, the situation fostered a blame culture, eroding professional relationships and cooperation, and consequently, service availability suffered.

The root of these misunderstandings stemmed from two main issues:

- It's comprehensive understanding of all IT systems and the significance of the alerts.

- The Support and Operations team's lack of detailed knowledge about IT systems, preventing them from interpreting alerts correctly and understanding the specific responsibilities within the IT department.

The resolution involved the IT team developing a process with several key sub-documents:

- An overview of IT systems and services for high-level understanding.

- A detailed description of each IT team's responsibilities.

- An explanation of the different components within IT systems and the rationale for their segregation.

- A guide to understanding alarms and warnings, including the significance of various alerts and appropriate responses.

Additionally, a clear process was established and documented, outlining the steps the Supervision & Monitoring team should follow upon detecting an issue, including internal technical service level agreements (SLAs) for response times.

Following the preparation of these documents, information exchange sessions and on-the-job training were conducted for the Supervision and Maintenance team.

The introduction of these measures led to the following improvements:

- The Supervision and Monitoring teams became more proficient and took greater responsibility in incident management.

- IT teams were alerted only for critical issues, enhancing efficiency.

- The quality of services improved and became more consistent.

- Team collaboration and cooperation significantly improved.

Key Takeaway from this case:

The importance of a supportive culture and effective communication was underscored. By providing detailed instructions, clarifications, and training, the organization fostered better teamwork and significantly enhanced the quality of its services.

~~ end of story ~~

5.7 Disaster Recovery And Business Continuity

In this chapter, I will briefly explore the definitions and key components of two critical processes: Disaster Recovery and Business Continuity.

Although they might not encompass the entirety of your duties, certain aspects of each process should be integral to the activities of a CIO.

What is Disaster Recovery?

Disaster Recovery (DR) in the IT domain refers to a set of policies, tools, and procedures that enable the recovery or continuation of vital technology infrastructure and systems following a natural or human-induced disaster.

Disaster recovery focuses specifically on IT or technology systems that support critical business functions, as opposed to business continuity, which involves keeping all essential aspects of a business running despite significant disruptions.

Purpose of Disaster Recovery:

The main goal of disaster recovery is to minimize downtime and data loss to ensure business continuity. By having a robust DR plan, organizations can:

- Ensure the integrity and availability of critical data and applications.

- Reduce the financial impact of downtime and data loss.

- Maintain customer trust and compliance with legal or regulatory obligations.

In summary, Disaster Recovery is a critical component of overall risk management and business continuity planning, ensuring that IT services can be restored as quickly and smoothly as possible after a disaster.

Key Components of Disaster Recovery:

- **Data Backup:** Regularly copying and archiving computer data so it can be accessed in the event of data deletion or corruption.

- **Recovery Objectives:** Defined by two key metrics:

    - **Recovery Time Objective (RTO):** The targeted duration of time and a service level within which a business process must be restored after a disaster in order to avoid unacceptable consequences associated with a break in business continuity.

    - **Recovery Point Objective (RPO):** The maximum tolerable period in which data might be lost from an IT service due to a major incident.

- **Disaster Recovery Plan (DRP):** A documented, structured approach with instructions for responding to unplanned incidents, which includes protecting and recovering data, hardware, and applications as well as ensuring that employees can communicate effectively in a crisis.

- **Testing:** Regular testing of the DRP to ensure its effectiveness and to make adjustments based on test outcomes and evolving business requirements.

- **Site Redundancy:** Having physical or cloud-based alternative sites where data and applications can be mirrored or backed up. These sites are typically classified as hot, warm, or cold:

    - **Hot Site:** A fully functional data center with hardware and software, personnel, and customer data, capable of resuming operations within a few hours.

    - **Warm Site:** A equipped data center that does not have customer data preloaded, but is otherwise ready to receive it and start operations within a few days.

- **Cold Site:** A facility where the necessary infrastructure (space, power, connectivity) exists but hardware, software, and data must be installed afresh.

What is Business Continuity?

Business Continuity (BC) refers to the processes, policies, and procedures that enable an organization to maintain essential functions or quickly resume them in the event of a major disruption, whether due to natural disasters, cyber-attacks, or other significant threats.

Unlike Disaster Recovery (DR), which is primarily focused on the recovery of IT systems and data after a disaster, Business Continuity encompasses a broader scope of planning to ensure the continuation of critical business operations.

Purpose of Business Continuity:

The primary goal of business continuity planning is to protect the organization in the event of an unexpected or potentially disruptive incident by:

- Ensuring the continuity of critical business operations.

- Minimizing financial loss and negative impacts on customers and stakeholders.

- Maintaining brand reputation and customer trust.

- Complying with regulatory requirements and industry standards.

Business Continuity is a holistic approach to organizational resilience, focusing on maintaining operational capabilities under adverse conditions and ensuring the organization can effectively recover from any disruption.

Key Components of Business Continuity:

- **Business Impact Analysis (BIA):** An essential part of BC planning, BIA involves identifying critical business functions and the impact that a disruption could have on them. This analysis helps prioritize resources and recovery strategies.

- **Risk Assessment:** Identifying potential threats and vulnerabilities that could impact the organization's ability to operate. This includes both internal and external risks.

- **Continuity Strategies:** Developing strategies to manage risk and ensure that key operations can continue with minimal downtime. These strategies may involve alternative processes, diversifying supply chains, or arranging for remote work capabilities.

- **Incident Response Plan:** A plan detailing the immediate steps to take in response to a disruption, including establishing a command structure, communication plans, and procedures for minimizing the impact.

- **Recovery Plans:** Detailed instructions for returning to normal operations after the initial response. This includes restoring IT operations, manufacturing processes, or other critical business functions.

- **Training and Testing:** Regular training for employees on their roles in business continuity plans, coupled with testing and drills to ensure plans are effective and that staff are prepared.

- **Maintenance and Review:** Continuous review and updates to the BC plan to reflect changes in the business environment, operational procedures, or after an incident review to improve future responses.

Difference between Business Continuity and Disaster Recovery:

The conceptual distinction between Business Continuity and Disaster Recovery is presented in the table below.

Aspect	Business Continuity (BC)	Disaster Recovery (DR)
Scope	Encompasses the entire organization, focusing on maintaining or quickly resuming critical business functions.	Primarily focuses on IT systems and data recovery to restore technology infrastructure after a disaster.
Objective	Minimize business operation disruptions and maintain essential functions during and after a disaster.	Quickly recover IT operations and data access to minimize downtime and support business functions.
Focus Areas	Includes human resources, facilities, supply chain, and communication, in addition to IT services.	Concentrates on IT infrastructure, applications, and data backup and restoration processes.

Table 3. **Core differences between Business Continuity and Disaster Recovery.**

To conclude this subsection, I would like to emphasize that regardless of whether your organization has Disaster Recovery (DR) or Business Continuity (BC) plans in place, a CIO should adopt similar practices to guarantee the secure operation of all IT components critical to the company's functionality.

To finalize this chapter, I would emphasize the following:

Regularly adjust processes according to evolving Business and Market conditions. Consider employing the PDCA (Plan-Do-Check-Act) methodology for continuous improvement.

Remember, effective processes evolve with changing landscapes.

Outline of Chapter 5: Manage Your Internal and External Processes

1. Service Level Agreements (SLAs)

   - **With Suppliers**: Establish clear, compliant agreements for hardware, software, and services. Educate the business on IT capabilities and limitations.

- **For Internal Clients**: Define responsibilities, escalation paths, response times, and communication methods for IT support.

- **For External Clients:** Tailor service quality and responsiveness based on regulatory or business needs, ensuring system responsiveness and security.

- **Technical SLA:** Applies to Datacenter elements like power and conditioning.

2. **Information Security** - from day 1 implement: information categorization, newcomer training, security rules implementation based on information categorization, various security policies, and strict access control.

3. **Change Management Process** - a clear, transparent process that addresses changes, assigns responsibility, establishes timelines, includes an escalation matrix, and integrates with the Roadmap process.

4. **Roadmap Process and Related Elements**

Understand and apply project management methodologies, including clear prioritization, planning, managing simultaneous projects and regular status meetings for roadmap delivery.

5. **Tools for Roadmap Management -** tools for managing the Roadmap are very useful but focus on the process over the tools.

6. **Monitoring and Support Processes** - implement robust Incident and Problem Management processes for effective support.

7. **Flexibility and readiness for change** - processes adjustments are crucial to responding to Business and Market changes.

8. **Safeguard continuous and secure operations** – consider implementing tools and procedures to safeguard IT ecosystems and ensure continuous business operations.

Your records: I encourage you to write down your conclusion / ideas / actions from this Chapter. This action will ensure that the information you get will have practical utilization.

Chapter 6. Build Your Team

In cultivating a professional and motivated team, CIOs should focus on building key values, communication, and key internal processes.

At every step, consider your "Vs" and Culture – long term Vision & Values, Culture of the Company and IT Culture - practice them through these activities.

Real-Life Story - Building your team with simple Cultural values.

I'm sharing a story from the early days of my management career. I was part of the IT division in a company that faced numerous challenges, including financial issues, organizational problems, and a risky position in the market.

A new CEO was appointed, and all members of the company's management team were convened for a meeting to acquaint ourselves with the new company leader.

Typically, a new leader spends around three months (90-100 days) to grasp the company's situation (akin to an IT assessment process, but broader) before taking significant leadership steps. During these initial months, we operated as usual: different departments and teams conflicted, and projects were slow to start, and even slower to implement due to these disputes. Each team or department viewed their work as paramount, often undermining the significance of others whenever possible.

Surprisingly, we considered such dynamics "normal". We recognized our contributions as significant but viewed the efforts of others as less so. Consequently, it was challenging to consider, adapt, or implement the ideas of others.

As mentioned, the CEO spent around three months assessing the situation. Then, at the beginning of the year—a time when we typically reviewed the previous year's results and discussed strategies or visions for the coming year—we had a common meeting.

However, this meeting deviated from the norm.

The meeting started in a familiar manner, but the latter half was entirely different. The new boss outlined his perception of the current situation, echoing my earlier description: conflicts, lack of commitment, absence of communication, no teamwork, reactive approaches, insufficient planning, a culture of blame, "ping-pong" behaviors, and indirect work, with employees constantly complaining to their direct managers.

This situation was clearly harmful to both the company and its teams.

He then introduced new company rules—a **new culture** upon which we would base our work:

- **Teamwork**: Achieve results together.

- **Proactiveness**: Move beyond reactive work.

- **Horizontal Collaboration**: People should work directly with their peers from other departments, bypassing the need for supervisory mediation.

- **No Blame Game or Complaining**: Address issues directly and attempt to resolve them. Escalate only if direct resolution fails.

He requested each manager to adhere to these rules and to disseminate the new culture throughout the company, encouraging everyone to adopt these new approaches.

Naturally, we were somewhat skeptical about the new rules, doubting that much would change. Nevertheless, we complied and began to integrate the new culture into our daily work.

Fast forward one year later: our market position had not only improved, but we had also become the leader, unreachable by our competitors.

The company had transformed into a complete and unified team!

What actually changed:

- The rules against complaining and "ping-pong" emails led us to address complex questions in meetings instead of lengthy email threads, significantly reducing our email backlog and resolving many issues.

- Proactiveness encouraged us to think ahead about improvements, new projects, or ways to support business departments in resolving issues.

- Horizontal collaboration allowed us to work with peers from other departments without constantly seeking managerial approval. This isn't to say actions shouldn't be communicated to managers, but rather, the work itself—responding to an email, organizing a meeting on a new project, explaining feasibility—didn't always require a manager's direct involvement.

The Takeaway from this case:

Often, we fear simplicity, but sometimes, simple principles need to guide our day-to-day work. Embracing a culture where we view ourselves as a team, value each other, and focus on solving issues rather than complaining, can empower a team to exceed expectations and achieve remarkable success.

~~ end of story ~~

To build the team you need Values and Culture, as well as clear processes.

Here are essential practices to consider.

6.1 Hiring Process

Hiring can be a "scary" process, as it involves bringing in new people, ensuring that the candidate meets your requirements, and hoping that the person will remain with the company and perform their duties effectively. Therefore, it's crucial to approach the hiring process carefully.

Here are some suggestions on how to achieve truly positive outcomes:

- Review candidate's CVs: Resumes/CVs should be reviewed by the CIO or a designated responsible individual to ensure a thorough assessment.

- Bypassing HR Hurdles: While involving HR in the hiring process, the technology-centric aspects should be overseen by those with a technical background to prevent misunderstandings.

- Efficient and Transparent Processes: Streamline the hiring process for professionals by making it transparent, efficient, and aligned with the team's needs.

Key point: as much as possible, try to reduce the timing between the interview and work offer, especially for key positions.

Real-life example about my hiring practice.

Hiring can be a significant challenge for many companies, particularly when it comes to recruiting IT professionals with both experience and a willingness to change jobs. While

HR teams are typically tasked with handling this process, based on my experience, relying solely on HR in the hiring process is a mistake.

In my managerial roles, I observed the struggles of other departments and IT management in securing the right professionals. Sometimes, the process took over a year to fill a position.

Here is how I approached this challenge:

- I collaborated with HR to ensure they played their part in preparing the Job Description, posting announcements, and undertaking recruitment tasks, such as searching social networks and liaising with other recruiters.

- All CVs received for a position were meticulously reviewed by either myself or a designated colleague from my team. We verified the candidates' experience, technical expertise, and suitability for the position. It was the first step!

- Following the CV review done by IT, potential candidates were selected, and HR then organized interviews. The interview process involved an initial meeting with HR (which is mandatory as an introduction for the new candidate), followed by a technical interview with either the technical team or me, depending on availability. These interviews were conducted on the same day. Technical interviews included both testing and general questions about experience and knowledge. During the testing period, no mobile phones or notebooks were allowed.

- For selected candidates, a security check was conducted by the designated Security responsible.

- Once the security check was successfully completed, a tailored job offer was extended to the candidate.

About the interview process:

- Throughout the interview process, we emphasized a professional attitude and kindness with each candidate.

- Punctuality was crucial, and it was essential to avoid adopting an authoritative attitude; instead, a polite demeanor was maintained.

- Providing comprehensive details about the company during the interview was considered crucial. Important information should not be withheld, as discovering vital details after joining can lead to dissatisfaction among employees.

About the salary negotiation, I took the following approach: if the candidate's requested salary is below the figure planned by the company, it was a practice to offer a higher salary. Many candidates may hesitate to ask for a higher salary initially, but providing a competitive salary upfront contributes to improved motivation.

Takeaways from this approach:

This approach to the interview and the candidate has proven effective, resulting in the successful hiring of numerous individuals who contributed significantly to the company's growth, benefiting both the organization and the individuals themselves.

~~ end of story ~~

6.2 Manage Continuous Learning - Hard And Soft Skills

Everything is evolving! You and your team need to possess the knowledge and skills to tackle the real challenges of today and tomorrow, rather than relying solely on what was learned yesterday. Therefore, fostering a culture of continuous learning is crucial both for the company as a whole and for every team member.

Consider the following two points to address this topic:

- **Training Plans:** Develop and sustain a comprehensive training plan based on team knowledge, business and technology trends, and essential soft skills to enhance teamwork, focus, and motivation.

- **Lead by Example:** Active participation in training fosters a culture of continuous Team members following their leader's commitment to learning.

6.3 Implement Salary Structure And Career Path.

Salaries for technology employees are a key point of motivation and a reflection of their value.

Therefore, consider these two aspects:

- **Market-Aligned Salaries:** Ensure that salaries align with market standards and the cost of living in the specific geographic location.

- **Balanced Compensation:** Design a system with components such as salary, performance evaluation, and bonuses, with clear visibility into potential career paths.

Salary grid **example**

Employee grade	Minimum knowledge	Salary range	Level up condition
Q&A Engineering team			
Junior 1	• Basic Knowledge of QA • Analytical thinking • Basic knowledge about Information Technology from both software and hardware perspective • Understanding of required tasks • Ability to learn fast	250–350	• During evaluation • Result of project
.....			
Middle 1		00-900	
......			
Senior 1,2,3, TL		1500-2500	
Development team			
Junior 1		300-400	
......			

Salary modification – once a year as rule (with possible exceptions). For Junior positions can be set - twice a year.

Table 4. Salary Grid Example.

6.4 Implement Motivational Systems

You and your team will encounter various situations, crises, issues, and successes. One element that will help you maintain the proper work attitude is your motivational strategy for each individual - a motivational system!

Consider implementing several of the approaches presented below.

- **Transparent Salary Grid:** Develop a visible salary grid based on position and level for each employee level, providing clarity on achievement expectations and potential salary increases.

- **Performance Evaluation System:** Establish a transparent system tied to the roadmap and strategy execution, with clear objectives and a link to the bonus system.

- **Bonus System Logic:** Align bonuses with positions, attributing higher percentages to higher positions to recognize their greater impact on company results.

- **Tailored Talent Management:** Create a specific talent management matrix for key team members, addressing individual motivational factors.

> *Real-life Case About This Motivational System.*

Motivation stands as a pivotal topic for every manager.

Over years of my experience, I've come to realize that motivation should not be short-term, such motivation inevitably fades away. It is essential to construct a long-term motivational engine or system.

While there are various motivational methods, my preference leans towards simplicity and clarity: basing motivation on an individual's identity, their actions, and their aspirations.

Hence, in most of the companies I've worked for, with each team and individual, I established a program grounded in:

- Salary
- Performance Evaluation
- Bonus

Let's delve into each topic separately:

Salary - While everyone appreciates a good salary, its motivating impact diminishes over time, often perceived as a routine payment for one's work.

Therefore, instead of a simple salary, we transform it into a Salary Grid & Career Path (an example of Salary Grid is Table 4.).

Formally executed by HR for the entire company, I utilized it as a vital component of the motivational system. The message conveyed was that this is a potential career path, providing each person with visibility on how they can progress in terms of position, knowledge, and salary increase.

(Note) Try to leverage existing elements within your company! Not every new idea necessitates new implementation or new components. A change in perspective, without manipulation, can significantly alter people's outlook.

Performance Evaluation - another tool typically managed by HR within each department.

This could become a futile task, consuming time without yielding meaningful results, if not executed properly, if not considered thoughtfully, or if the focus is solely on the bonus component rather than the individual.

I use Performance Evaluation as a tool to:

- Communicate with each individual about personal growth.

- Communicate about company strategy, emphasizing being part of something significant.

- Communicate about the success of the company, team, and individual.

- Engage in open and direct discussions about areas for improvement.

Even without a substantial bonus attached to this process, individuals understand that they are valued, their work is appreciated, their concerns are acknowledged, and efforts to facilitate their growth are supported.

The final segment of this motivational system is the bonus part.

Certainly, when it comes to monetary rewards, having an approved budget is crucial. Not every time was it sizable enough to meet my desire to recognize the team, but here's the key - honesty and genuine care make even a small bonus highly valuable.

As a Result:

People were eager to grow, with the growth path clearly visible to each of them. They worked as a team, translating into more success for the team, the company, and for each individually. Their willingness to introduce new ideas and adopt fresh approaches was a testament to the growth they experienced.

Takeaway from this story: Motivation should be grounded in a long-term approach. Cultivating a culture of care, utilizing standard elements of our work with a caring approach, allows the construction of a robust motivational tool. There's no need to create something new each time; a consistent and thoughtful approach motivates individuals to work and grow.

~~ end of story ~~

I need to highlight something about the bonus program.

The example I provided might not be applicable across all companies or industries.

You could adopt various methodologies, such as:

- Conducting performance evaluations for employees and assigning bonuses quarterly - to enhance motivation and focus, whereas for managers, performance evaluations and bonuses could be annual to encourage long-term actions and a focus on company results.

- Planning bonuses for the successful implementation of significant projects.

- Allocating bonuses for achieving strong results at the year's end.

Regardless of the performance evaluation and bonus system you develop, ensure it is relevant to your team's work and motivates each individual to contribute as part of the team.

6.5 Manage Properly Communication And Meetings

Effective communication is essential in every aspect of your work.

When properly managed, it ensures that irrespective of the circumstances, teamwork and performance remain unaffected.

- **Open Communication:** Maintain open and regular communication with teams and individual team members.
- **Mandatory Meetings:**
  - **Regular 1-to-1 performance evaluation meetings**, emphasizing constructive feedback – at least 2 times a year.
  - **Department-wide meetings** to set the stage for performance evaluations, discuss company strategy and outline departmental priorities - at least 2 times a year.
  - **Weekly meetings with direct reports** to share updates and ensure everyone has a voice.
  - **Weekly project meetings** with key team members to evaluate projects status and discuss new ideas.
- **Regular meetings with other department managers or directors** for cross-functional communication – the frequency can be monthly unless a more frequent cadence is deemed necessary.
- **Ad-hoc Meetings:** Conduct meetings as needed, such as project evaluations, crises, celebrations, and 1-to-1 sessions with individuals who require support or have underperformed.

Remember, the success of your team relies on adaptable and responsive leadership. Keep processes dynamic, aligning them with changing business and market dynamics.

Outline of Chapter 6: Build Your Team

1. Hiring Process Enhancements: Refine the hiring process to make it transparent and efficient, ensuring the right fit for the team while reducing the time from interview to job offer.

2. Promoting Continuous Learning: Keep focus on continuous learning through developing comprehensive training plans and leading by example.

3. Salary Structure and Career Paths: Align salaries with market standards and provide clear visibility of career progression paths to motivate and retain talent.

4. Implementing Motivational Systems: Beyond salary, enhance motivation with a performance evaluation system aligned with company strategy, impact-based rewards, and personalized talent management to meet individual motivational needs.

5. Effective Communication and Meeting Management: Ensure effective communication through open dialogue, regular individual, and team meetings.

Your records: I encourage you to write down your conclusion / ideas / actions from this Chapter. This action will ensure that the information you get will have practical utilization.

Chapter 7. Manage Technology

While this guide won't delve into intricate analyses of software, data center versus cloud options, or the selection of specific databases, its focus is on providing practical insights for proper technology management.

Here are key considerations.

7.1 Manage The Borders Of I T

As CIO, you are responsible for managing the company's technology.

Typically, there are two areas of technology management:

- **Internal**: This refers to the technology used within the company, such as IT equipment, software, licenses, etc.

- **External**: This pertains to technology provided by partners, including the technology solutions your company receives, alongside contracts and Service Level Agreements (SLAs).

Before delving into details for each area, I will share a real-life experience of managing the external aspect.

Real-life case - a crucial collaboration between IT and Purchasing from day one.

On this subject, I'm sharing insights from a remarkable venture I undertook at the company – launching a new Telecom Operator in an entirely new country, a complete Greenfield Start-up. This endeavor presented a unique market with its complexity, advantages, and challenges, offering IT professionals an ideal platform to create from scratch, ensuring everything from equipment to technology and processes aligned seamlessly.

Within this dynamic environment, one of my key responsibilities as CIO was to purchase IT equipment, covering user devices (PCs, notebooks, monitors, etc.) to Datacenter IT equipment (network gear, servers, storage, etc.). I want to underscore the critical role played by the Purchasing team in such challenging scenarios. Even for adept IT professionals equipped with a comprehensive understanding of needs, architectural expertise, and a readiness to organize purchases, collaboration with a Purchasing team is necessary due to various considerations:

- **Building Strong Business Relationships:**

- Partnering with a vendor requires establishing lasting business relationships to ensure responsibilities are fulfilled effectively.

- **Beyond the Price War:**

- The allure of low prices during a "price war" can be misleading. Long-term considerations such as support, parts replacements, and warranty expenses necessitate a thorough evaluation of the Total Cost of Ownership (TCO) over 3 or 5 years.

- **Navigating Tricky Suppliers:**

- In a new market, dealing with unknown suppliers necessitates caution. Purchasing teams act as a safeguard, enforcing compliance with requirements and preventing potential pitfalls like special tricks or shortcuts.

Our approach involved initiating an RFP (Request for Proposal), where Purchasing took charge of the process. This involved crafting RFP specifications based on technical and business requirements, sending them to potential service providers, and evaluating proposals based on predetermined conditions and timelines.

During the relatively brief RFP duration, spanning approximately a month due to the urgency of the situation, our focus encompassed the following key actions:

- Conducting meetings with potential suppliers.

- Analyzing the offers and accompanying documentation.

- Scrutinizing their actual capabilities vis-à-vis their proposals.

At first glance, all seemed to be more or less professional, capable of fulfilling our requests.

However, through our collaboration with the Purchasing team, we unearthed critical insights:

- **Identification of "Fake Companies":** uncovering several entities operating as part of a larger conglomerate engaged in deceptive competition and pricing tactics. Prohibited by RFP rules, these companies were coordinating proposals within their group, leading to disqualification. This underscored our commitment to finding a partner rather than merely opting for the cheapest prices.

- **Warranty and Support Deception:** unearthing a company falsely claiming compliance with our warranty and support requirements, despite having a small support team of only four engineers presented a substantial risk, particularly for services that rely on local engineers.

- **Reluctance to Maintain Spare Parts Stock:** identifying companies unwilling to uphold a stock of spare parts, a crucial This not only aligned with our needs but also was easily organized by sourcing from larger suppliers like HP or DELL, who willingly included spare parts in larger quantities.

The challenge extended beyond meeting requirements; it delved into the willingness of potential partners to share risks. We emphasized our quest for a partner genuinely prepared to collaborate on risk-sharing.

Following numerous meetings and calls, we eventually narrowed down our choices to two players with compelling offers and favorable Total Cost of Ownership (TCO) considerations—a pivotal factor in our purchasing strategy, emphasizing the importance of evaluating costs over time.

Selecting a supplier, accepting their offer, and initiating the delivery process became the next critical steps.

The date on the calendar was December 25th. In the country

where we were working, it was not a holiday. However, one of the two pre-selected suppliers explained that they would not work on the purchase offer because their partners in the EU were on holiday. As a result, they stated that they would commence work after January 3rd of the following year.

The decision was made easier when another supplier demonstrated a readiness to commence work, even during this holidays period - an indication of a partner willing to make sacrifices, understand our needs, and potentially evolve into a valuable long-term collaborator for our company.

As a result, we have found a partner who not only delivered all the necessary items on time but has also proven to be one of the best partners in the country over the years!

Key Insights and Takeaways from this case:

- **Collaboration Between IT and Purchasing:** successful outcomes require seamless collaboration between IT and Purchasing to ensure all conditions are met.

- **Specialized Tools and Knowledge:** purchasing teams possess unique tools and knowledge crucial for thoroughly assessing potential partners beyond their ability to deliver equipment.

- **TCO Over Initial Cost:** evaluating offers should extend beyond the immediate Understanding TCO over 3 or 5 years provides a comprehensive view for decision-making.

- **Choosing a Partner, Not Just a Supplier:** recognizing the value of a long-term partnership over a mere "equipment delivery" arrangement is paramount for sustained success.

This experience underscores the significance of a robust partnership between IT and Purchasing, leveraging their respective strengths for informed decision-making and long-term success.

~~ end of story ~~

Let's delve now into the details of both domains: Internal and External.

- Internally:

Establish clear policies with the CEO and CxOs regarding "Who is responsible for Company Technology purchasing/management/selection?" to prevent conflicts, cost increases, and incidents.

Ensure collaboration with non-Technology leaders, especially in the context of cloud solutions, avoiding siloed decision-making and potential integration challenges. Agree that the IT department is responsible for setting requirements, participating in selection processes, and maintaining all software and IT hardware solutions.

- Externally:

Identify trusted partners to share responsibility for specific aspects, like warranty and support of equipment or solutions. Select suppliers for PC/Notebooks, office IT equipment, servers, and other IT equipment with proper RFI (Request for Information)/RFP (Request for Proposal) processes.

Define contractual conditions for equipment maintenance, warranty, and post-warranty support with the chosen partners. Utilize the IT purchasing process and template to select reliable partners.

To effectively oversee external suppliers and partners, establishing robust relationships with the Purchasing team is imperative.

The Purchasing team plays a pivotal role in the IT procurement process, from vendor selection to contract negotiation and ongoing supplier management. Building strong relationships with Procurement fosters an environment of cooperation, where expectations are clearly communicated and aligned with organizational objectives.

7.2 Have Key Technical Knowledge Inside Your Team.

Develop in-house expertise to ensure control over systems, challenge partners effectively, and enhance service delivery. Create a team of professionals with knowledge in configuring, recovering from incidents, and managing systems, even if external partners handle most responsibilities.

---
real-life case about how full IT Outsourcing was leading to a big failure.

When I worked for an international company, one of our affiliates decided to outsource IT to an external vendor. (as the sub-chapter say "keep your key staff inside the team" I'm personally and professionally totally against such approach... but let's see what happened.)

The reasons were quite clear:

- Difficulty in finding and hiring good talents.

- Difficulty in maintaining the necessary number of specialists and certificates per system (due to many systems).

- Difficulty in properly maintaining the architecture (due to many systems).

Of course, the difficulty was mainly related to the cost of hiring, certifications, and retaining IT staff.

Even though the company was performing well with revenue and its position in the market, its IT costs were higher compared to other affiliates and the average IT costs vs. revenue KPI.

They decided to 'almost' fully outsource IT to an external supplier!

After 5 years of IT outsourcing, the company's operations were in complete disarray regarding collaboration with IT. Almost nothing related to IT was under control.

What does it mean IT was not under control?

Marketing wants to implement some new offers or new products. Market in any domain has a lot of competition, therefore such projects to implement new things are very frequent, can be 50 to 100 per year or more.

If the company is not launching this kind of offers, services, and products, it is going to have very hard time… because customers may leave and go to a competitor easily.

Imagine, from a business standpoint they are doing all needed for these projects, but when it comes to the IT, the department which must deliver the project, it is becoming very difficult to get the clarity: what is the feasibility? what will be the timing of delivery? what will be the cost and impact on other offers?

Because of this unclear situation, almost all the teams and departments are suffering: not clear when Customer service is going to train their agents, not clear when Sales will train their staff, not clear when to work on the PR messages, not clear when finance needs to prepare and analyze the impact of implemented project on the revenue, and so on.

Certainly, for a company reliant on IT-delivered services, this chaos has given rise to financial and marketing considerations as well.

After this experience of losing control over IT, they understood it was a mistake.

They finally decided to move back a significant part of IT responsibilities, internalizing a key part of IT.

Takeaway from this story:

Every technology company must keep key IT/technology

personnel internally. Some parts of IT may be outsourced, but control should be kept internally.

~~end of story~~

You might be wondering how to identify the knowledge that should be retained within the team.

Here is a practical way to determine which knowledge should be kept inside the IT team, based on my experience.

It is essential to maintain internal expertise in the following domains:

- **Used system software**: For any system software your team uses, such as Microsoft or Linux technologies, it's crucial to have in-house administration expertise, including all the versions in use. (Sys admins, DevOps, SREs)

- **Used databases**: For any database technology your team utilizes, you need to have internal knowledge on managing these databases. (DBAs)

- **Used hardware:** Knowledge of managing the hardware you use is necessary.

- **Used IT equipment:** Expertise in any other IT equipment should be maintained internally. You may need to engage additional resources from partners if you have a large quantity of equipment or if it's geographically distributed.

- (note) Utilizing external partners for support of your various IT equipment does not eliminate the need for internal expertise.

- **Used business software (like Billing, CRM, ERP, HRM, etc.):** Primarily for configuration and support. If your company uses any business software, you need internal engineers trained to manage this software at the level provided by the supplier, at minimum for configuration and support.

- (note) Some suppliers offer development capabilities

within their systems. Whether to keep an internal team for development or to purchase development services from the supplier or its partners is a decision that depends on pricing, time to market, etc.

- Cloud business software: There are two scenarios for such software:

- If the software is used completely independently, the IT team may not need any knowledge of this software.

- If there is any integration with the software, the IT team will need to have someone internally responsible for managing the software and its integration part.

Why is it so important to maintain internal expertise in these key areas?

Let's see two practical cases are described below: one involves an unprepared individual dealing with an incident that needed to be resolved with a partner, and the second case involves a person who was professionally prepared to handle the situation.

Case 1 (no expertise inside the team)

An issue arose with one of our services. The individual tasked with addressing the problem was not sufficiently trained and lacked a deep understanding of the system. They were unfamiliar with the location of the logs, the software version, and recent changes made to the system.

During the incident, this person contacted the support service of our partner, which provided these services. This person reported that the service was malfunctioning and requested assistance to restore it. However, the call lacked evidence and detail, leading the partner's support service to ask several questions, such as the software version, the database status, and the last time an upgrade, update, or patch was applied. Receiving no constructive responses, they requested that our engineer sends an email with this detailed information.

Clearly, this type of interaction resulted in additional time spent gathering the requested information. Instead of immediately addressing the issue, the partner requested further details. The situation was not urgent for them because they were awaiting a formal report of the issue, not just a call reporting a problem. Typically, it takes at least 15-30 minutes (sometimes up to an hour) to collect all the necessary information. Then providing the information late often led to back-and-forth communication, such as "Some information is missing" or "The provided information is insufficient." Consequently, the partner or supplier began addressing the issue later ranging from 15 minutes to an hour.

This meant that your customers could not use the system and its functionalities, while the supplier awaited further information instead of promptly dealing with the issue.

Case 2 (professional attitude and knowledge)

The second case highlights the importance of having the right expertise within the IT team.

Our engineers are responsible for all business applications. They are knowledgeable about versions and details (e.g., OS, Database), and they keep track of the last upgrades, updates, or patches applied, even if these actions were not performed by them. They monitor the software after any work is done by a supplier.

Now, imagine the same issue arises, and the system is not working. According to the Service Level Agreement (SLA), you need to call the supplier and send a Trouble Ticket (TT). The person responsible for the system, or your engineer, gathers all the necessary information—including versions, details, and the history of recent work—and sends the TT to the supplier.

Upon calling the supplier, this individual only needs to mention that there is an issue, and the details are included in the TT.

In this scenario, the supplier begins working on the TT immediately. Furthermore, if any information is missing from your ticket, they will not halt their investigation but will either check it themselves or ask your engineer for clarification.

So, how do you think the supplier's attitude in case 1 and case 2 will differ?

Obviously, in the first case, as the information is incomplete, the supplier spends time without a concrete case to solve.

In the second case, the supplier starts immediately and adopts a much more professional attitude towards resolving the issue.

The key takeaway from point 7.2 - importance of maintaining critical expertise within an IT team across various domains, including system software, databases, hardware, IT equipment, and business software (including cloud-based solutions).

Having this expertise not only ensures operational efficiency and effectiveness in managing and supporting these systems but also significantly impacts the team's ability to respond to and resolve incidents swiftly and effectively.

7.3 Selection Of Proper Architecture/Technical Solution

Implement a straightforward but rigorous process with strict requirements for selecting the appropriate architecture and technical solutions.

For example, each and any change in the architecture must be:

- Checked versus licensing compliance.

- Checked versus interoperability with all core elements and non-core but critical elements.

- Checked on a test environment.

- Validated by [create a list of validators].

- Modifications Communicated clearly with all the possible actions which must be done for the implementation and rollback.

The selection and approval process can involve various practices and tools.

One example is the SWOT analysis, which stands for Strengths, Weaknesses, Opportunities, and Threats. A SWOT analysis offers a high-level overview to aid in the decision-making process for selecting an IT solution, considering both internal capabilities and external possibilities. Refer to the example in Table 5 below.

Table 5. Example of SWOT analysis - select the IT tool X.

SWOT analysis for implementing the Tool X	
Strength	**Weaknesses**
- Customizability to fit	- Initial costs and

specific business needs - Potential integration with existing systems - Can improve efficiency and productivity - Access to vendor support and updates	potential for unexpected expenses - Time required for implementation and training - Risk of disruption during the transition period - Possible compatibility issues with existing infrastructure
Opportunities	**Threats**
- Ability to gain competitive advantage through improved operations - Access to new technologies and innovations - Potential to scale and adapt as the business grows - Opportunity to streamline processes and reduce manual work	- Changes in technology may render the solution obsolete - Risk of vendor lock-in and dependency - Security vulnerabilities and data privacy concerns - Potential resistance to change within the organization

While tools are not crucial for this process, they can enhance visualization and aid in making informed decisions. These include presentation tools (PowerPoint, Slides), documentation tools (Confluence, SharePoint), and various reporting tools (Excel, Sheets, BI solutions).

7.4 Monitoring Tools And Processes Are Mandatory

Incorporate monitoring tools to keep systems under control, detect issues promptly, and ensure proactive management.

Additionally, consider implementing alert mechanisms for real-time notifications, regularly analyze performance metrics to identify trends, and establish automated reporting for a comprehensive overview of system health.

A real-life story about the importance of proper Monitoring and cooperation of IT with the monitoring teams is presented in point 5.6.

7.5 Reporting And B I - Manage Them Properly

Implement a robust reporting and business intelligence strategy, emphasizing "common" approaches for information reporting. Insist on a unified understanding of key indicators across systems and reports, establishing a shared "one truth" layer.

For example, define what constitutes an active or inactive customer to align reporting metrics.

Real-case - an example of implementing one-truth layer on top of our data.

The case itself is simple, but it was very challenging to execute.

One of my teams was responsible for developing and delivering reports and BI for the entire company.

We had a good process for handling reporting requests, and the team performed well in delivering reports and providing a BI solution for different business departments.

When a report was required, each business department had its own KPIs, its own terminology, and even the understanding of KPIs was quite specific for each department.

And what happened was the following: once, when presenting to the CEO, one department was showing its figures/KPIs, and another department was presenting its figures/KPIs. What we, as IT, didn't see at the time was that when they (business colleagues) were presenting the figures to the CEO, they were using similar KPIs, BUT the figures were different!!!

Of course, it was not acceptable to have "incorrect" figures, so they addressed the issue to IT - asking why the figure was wrong.

As you get it, the figures were not "incorrect," but the name of the KPI was similar with different figures.

After our internal analysis, we understood that even though they were using the "same terminology for their KPIs," the formulas they were using for one or another KPI were different.

Example: KPI - active customer

For Marketing, it meant: "a customer who is in an active phase, using services at least x times per month."

For IT, it meant: "a customer who is active in the system" (such a customer can be in any commercial status but is still incurring the license cost).

The problem was critical - reports and BI are used to decide on the next steps, define the company's strategy! If the figures are not aligned - the strategy is impossible to follow and implement!

Therefore, a project was launched to:

- Define KPI names and formulas based on company needs.

- Agree on common terminology between departments.

- Have a BI and Reporting layer where all the data would be aggregated and located - used for most of the company's reporting.

One of the key points: the project was led by Finance, as they held the responsibility for the company's reporting.

(Note): the result of any project depends on who is leading it, and its responsibilities and commitment to this project.

After several months of analysis, discussions, and meetings, the final specifications of how the KPIs must be calculated, how they have to be visible, and how they have to be used were finalized.

Here I want to emphasize the importance of Interdepartmental communication and cooperation: in most cases, each department has its own strategy and priorities. And they should be focused on reaching results. When working with IT to request a software tool or report, they consider this as part of their "reaching their results" work. And they do not see the dependency of similar tools or reports globally on the whole company. But it is visible by IT, by the CIO. Therefore, the role of CIO is to communicate with all leaders of business departments and with CEO in order to facilitate the implementation of interdepartmental interaction. One case is reporting, another case can be a common ERP or CRM solution. The more departments are communicating and cooperating, the more efficient the work of IT will be - to deliver solutions which will be useful for the whole company is much better than to deliver unique and scattered solutions for each department separately.

From the IT side, we were part of almost all the meetings to understand and be in line with what could be requested.

(Note): the key point of IT participation was the following: even if almost everything is possible on the IT side, everything has a cost. Our responsibility was to find an optimal and efficient way to get, process, and provide the data properly and on time.

Then we started the development of this layer, and in several months, it was ready.

The first month after launch brought fantastic results - the new layer brought clarity to most of the KPIs, figures, and reports used in the company by different departments.

The business was confidently using this data to build the Strategy and Roadmap.

Takeaway from this case: To be a data-driven company, it is crucial to invest in the definition of KPIs and define how the information is used to see the company results and how it is used to create the company strategy.

~~ *end of story* ~~

7.6 Information Security

Last but not least, Information Security is not just a separate domain. Information Security must be an integral part of each component listed above, and much more.

If other domains may not impact the whole company, this domain is impacting and is influenced by each employee independent of where the employee works.

We've discussed the importance of Information Security measures in the Process Chapter, in sub-chapter 5.2.

To implement and manage Information Security it is important to:

- Cooperate with Information Security team (if such team of Department exist).

- Cooperate with HR and prepare information security information regarding using company data, company information resources.

- Prepare a comprehensive presentation with main Information Security points: password rules, access and sharing rules, email ethics, etc. to be part of initial handbook provided to each employee.

7.7 Manage Your I T K P Is

The work of a CIO and the IT department overall is multifaceted, encompassing various levels or domains such as:

- Managing equipment
- Managing software
- Providing services to both internal and external clients
- Ensuring SLAs (Service Level Agreements) and effective Incident Management
- Promoting continuous learning
- Ensuring proper utilization of financial resources
- Among others...

To evaluate and demonstrate how the IT department is managing most of its responsibilities, as a CIO, you need to implement an IT KPIs (Key Performance Indicators) reporting system. This system should include the most important KPIs for both you and the company, calculate them, and present them.

Given that KPIs may vary across different companies or domains, I recommend following the logic of asking: **"Which services am I providing as IT?":**

- If implementing projects, then project delivery KPIs should be included.

- If budget is allocated to these projects, then a KPI for spending should be established.

- If providing network for the company office, what is the network's availability?

- If responsible for the availability of production systems, what is their availability?

This list is not exhaustive; it's merely an example to illustrate the logic.

To perform this exercise, you don't need a perfect list from other companies or industries. You can create your own KPIs list by following the simple logic mentioned above. Then, work on and analyze this list, implementing logical changes where needed. You may add some KPIs when you see a need.

It's crucial to have KPIs that focus on IT efficiency both internally and for Business.

Below is a table with examples of different KPIs, their descriptions, and value ranges.

Table 6. Example of IT KPIs.

#	KPI Name	Understanding	Expected Value
1	System Uptime	Measures the percentage of time IT systems are available and operational.	99.5% - 99.999%
2	Mean Time to Repair (MTTR)	The average time it takes to repair a system or component after a failure.	1-4 hours
3	Mean Time Between Failures (MTBF)	The average time between system failures.	300+ hours
4	First Call Resolution Rate	Percentage of incidents resolved during the first interaction with support.	70% - 90%
5	Help Desk Ticket Resolution Time	The average time it takes to resolve a help desk support ticket.	< 24 hours
6	Network Latency	The time it takes for a data packet to	< 150 milliseconds

		travel from source to destination.	
7	Application Load Time	The time it takes for an application to become fully usable after launch.	< 2 seconds
8	Customer Satisfaction Score (CSAT)	Measures user satisfaction with IT services on a scale.	70% - 90%
9	IT Project Completion Rate	Percentage of IT projects completed on time.	85% - 95%
10	IT Budget Variance	The difference between the budgeted and actual IT spending.	±10%
11	Cost Per Ticket	The average cost of resolving a support ticket.	$15 - $50
12	Percentage of IT Budget Spent on Innovation	The portion of the IT budget allocated to new projects and innovation.	15% - 25%
13	Security Incidents per Year	The number of recorded security breaches or incidents per year.	0 - 5

As mentioned earlier, this KPI list is an example - you need to tailor them based on your IT team's responsibilities & services.

The expected values provided here are indicative and should be customized based on the organization's operational standards, industry benchmarks, and strategic objectives. Regular review and adjustment of these KPIs and their target values are crucial to ensure they remain aligned with the organization's evolving goals and challenges.

In summary, effective technology management involves a combination of internal and external collaboration, cultivating in-house expertise, selecting appropriate solutions, implementing monitoring tools, and establishing standardized reporting practices. These strategies collectively contribute to a well-managed and sustainable technology ecosystem.

Outline of this Chapter 7: Manage Technology

1. Manage IT Borders Internally and Externally: Concentrate on defining clear roles for technology management within the company and with external partners, including the establishment of robust SLAs for each area.

2. Maintain Key Technical Knowledge In-House: Internal expertise is crucial for challenging partners and enhancing service delivery.

3. Rigorous Selection of Architecture/Technical Solutions: Implement a process with strict requirements for selecting appropriate technology solutions, including compliance checks, interoperability verification, and thorough testing before implementation.

4. Implement Monitoring Tools and Processes: Implement monitoring tools and establish alert mechanisms for early issue detection and proactive management, along with regular performance analysis to maintain systems' health.

5. Standardize Reporting and Integrate Information Security: Develop a unified reporting and business intelligence strategy that aligns with company standards. Implement integrated information security standards.

6. Tailored IT KPI Reporting - Tailor you IT KPI reporting system. It aids in evaluating and demonstrating the effectiveness across various domains.

Your records: I encourage you to write down your conclusion / ideas / actions from this Chapter. This action will ensure that the information you get will have practical utilization.

RADU SPATARU

Chapter 8. Manage IT Budget

As highlighted in Chapter I, the IT budget is a pivotal tool enabling organizations to allocate resources effectively, prioritize initiatives, and ensure the IT department aligns with the technological needs of the business.

The budget for an IT department constitutes the financial plan encompassing anticipated expenses related to information technology functions within an organization. It spans various aspects of IT, encompassing hardware and software purchases, the acquisition of new software and licenses, infrastructure maintenance, personnel costs, training, cybersecurity measures, and other expenditures associated with managing and enhancing the organization's technological capabilities.

Given that CIOs typically lack a financial background, personal and organizational investments in knowledge are crucial for adept budget management.

Real-life Case: Failure in Budget Planning and Its Serious Impact.

This is a real-life case from my experience where a failure in proper budget planning led to a significant crisis affecting the company's operations.

Every year, one of our budget exercises involved capacity planning for the upcoming year. In our process, the business forecasted all relevant figures and technical teams conducted standard capacity planning exercises based on these projections. For equipment or software requiring upgrades, we meticulously planned the budget through multiple iterations, leaving no points unnoticed.

As described in this chapter, the budget was typically approved by the end of November. No changes were accepted after this point until the first budget review meeting.

Fast-forward to a hot summer day. I received a call from my team one Saturday reporting an issue in the data center—servers were shutting down due to problems with the air conditioning system. I, along with colleagues from various teams, rushed to the site to address the problem.

The company's services were down!
When company services are down, it becomes a highly stressful situation for all departments and the clients: stores are overwhelmed with customers inquiring when the issue will be resolved, customer service is flooded with calls asking the same question. To add more complexity – people within the company are contacting each other to find out when and how this will be resolved. Some, more stressed than others, may start arguments and so on.

Upon reaching the data center, we discovered that one of the three air conditioning systems had failed, and the remaining two were unable to maintain the required temperature. This caused the servers, including those hosting applications and databases, to automatically shut down due to overheating.

We improvised a solution by opening doors and introducing additional fans to cool the data center. After about an hour, the temperature began to drop, and we were able to restart the services. The faulty conditioning system was repaired later that day.

The incident lasted around 3 to 4 hours, significantly impacting our services and damaging the company's image. Post-recovery, we conducted an incident analysis, including a root cause analysis, and devised measures to prevent such incidents in the future.

What became evident was that this incident could have been avoided if the fourth air conditioning system had been purchased and installed before the summer began.

Upon reflection, we understood that the team responsible for planning the capacity of power and air conditioning systems failed to include the fourth system in the budget. Furthermore, during the first-quarter budget review in April, they once again overlooked its inclusion. In April, the issue was aggravated by the challenge of including something over-budget during the review. Typically, securing approval for a budget increase required extensive discussions with the CEO and CFO, and this exercise was not conducted effectively. Their initial request to include the fourth air conditioning system during the budget review was declined, and unfortunately, they didn't pursue it further.

Takeaway from this story:

Properly conducting capacity management and budget planning exercises is crucial. Additionally, it's important to acknowledge personal mistakes and persist in pursuing necessary changes, even if the initial request faces obstacles. When each team conducts its responsibilities diligently and rectifies mistakes, the company will experience fewer incidents and issues, contributing to its overall success and financial well-being.

~~ end of story ~~

The budgeting process generally involves two main phases: Budget Planning and Budget Review.

Below we will examine each of them.

8.1 Budget Planning

As discussed in Chapter III, a solid strategy forms the basis for effective budget planning. Following a well-constructed strategy, the subsequent step is budget development, requiring financial resources for both new initiatives and ongoing operational and support costs.

IT budgets usually have two primary categories:

- **CAPEX (Capital Expenditures):** Covers planned purchases of new infrastructure, licenses, systems, etc. Costs are estimated based on current expenses with a safety margin considering country-specific factors and historical price changes.

- **OPEX (Operational Expenditures):** Involving support contracts, SLAs, operational costs, training, and staff While costs are generally clearer than in CAPEX, collaboration with the Finance department is imperative for advice on pricing changes, exchange rate fluctuations, etc.

Budget planning typically starts three months before the year-end, with the final approval of the next year's budget around the end of November to early December.

During the budget planning exercise, the IT department receives capacity forecasts from various business departments. Subsequently, these figures are utilized to strategically plan the essential budgetary components for projects, capacity upgrades, supplier upgrades and updates, and other pertinent aspects.

8.2 Budget Review

Regular quarterly checks of the budget are considered good practice. The budget planned for Q1 is scrutinized against real expenses, any variations are explained and re-planned, and the budget file is updated accordingly. Depending on market challenges, some budget parts may be adjusted or deferred during this process.

In certain instances, unforeseen investments may arise during budget reviews due to company situations and market challenges.

In conclusion, effective budget management is an integral aspect of CIO responsibilities.

Mismanagement can hinder the ability to provide expected solutions, maintain service levels, hire personnel, and provide necessary training and materials. Continuous monitoring of costs and collaboration with finance counterparts for regular updates on extra-budget, over-budget, and under-budget cases is essential for successful IT budget governance.

8.3 IT Budget Domains

Let's now look at the possible items for an IT budget.

This table offers a general overview of how IT budget items can be categorized as CAPEX (Capital Expenditures) or OPEX (Operating Expenses).

Table 7. IT Budget - CAPEX.

CAPEX Domains	Short Description of Domains
Hardware Purchases	All IT equipment, from personal computers to Data center equipment (sometimes it may include mobile devices if they are used as IT equipment)
- Servers	
- Networking equipment	
- Storage devices	
- Personal computers and laptops	
- Mobile devices for employees	
Software Acquisitions	New Software acquisition of Customer software development
- One-time license purchases	
- Custom software development	
Building Infrastructure	All the infrastructure related to the Building and Datacenter
- Data center construction/ modification	

- Cabling and networking infrastructure	
Major Software Upgrades	Upgrades of existing software which are not part of software monthly or yearly support.
- Large-scale software implementation	
Intangible Assets	Specific assets like Intellectual properly
- Software patents and copyrights	
Project Specific Costs	here you can include all the projects from the Roadmap (Business and IT projects)
- Costs associated with major IT projects, not falling into yearly operational costs	

Now that we have an understanding of what is included in CAPEX, let's examine the main domains of OPEX in the IT budget:

Table 8. IT Budget - OPEX.

OPEX Domains	Short Description of Domains
Software Licenses (recurring fees)	All the payments which are monthly or yearly as part of you purchasing agreement
- Cloud Services (e.g., AWS, Azure)	
- SaaS subscriptions (e.g., Salesforce)	
Maintenance and Support	all the contracts of support and maintenance.

Contracts	
- Software support and updates	
- Hardware maintenance and repairs	
Utilities	Monthly services like Utilities, Internet service cost, Equipment maintenance
- Electricity for data centers/IT equipment	
- Internet service fees	
Salaries and Benefits	Salaries, Bonuses, Training cost of IT staff
- IT staff salaries	
- Training and professional development	
Cloud Services (operational usage)	Recurring cost of Cloud services
- Compute, storage, and data transfer costs	
Outsourcing Services	Specific services used to provide IT support.
- IT support and managed services	
- Consulting services	
Travel and Expenses	Travel and Expenses for work purposes (duty work, training)
- Travel related	

| to IT operations, such as vendor meetings or training | |

In some companies, the approach to cloud-based services or long-term licenses can be different. For example, all long-term cloud-based solutions, paid monthly or yearly, may then be capitalized, as they are considered part of your infrastructure.

Similarly, some software licenses might be capitalized if they provide benefits over several years and meet the organization's capitalization criteria.

8.4 The Strategic Essence Of I T Spending

Typically, the IT budget constitutes a significant portion of the company budget.

Naturally, there are many questions from business leaders about why IT is so costly.

Therefore, it falls within the CIO's role to openly discuss with business managers in the company and explain precisely what each budget element entails, its cost, and the benefits the company derives from it.

Here are some fundamental principles concerning the IT budget and its value:

1. Digital Transformation and Innovation:

Businesses are constantly undergoing digital transformation to stay competitive. This involves the adoption of new technologies, processes, and business models. Innovation requires investment in cutting-edge technology, research and development, and new systems that can streamline operations, enhance customer experiences, and open new revenue streams. These initiatives are essential for growth but come with significant costs.

2. Infrastructure and Maintenance:

The backbone of any organization's IT capabilities is its infrastructure, which includes data centers, networks, servers, and cybersecurity measures. Building, maintaining, and regularly updating this infrastructure to ensure reliability, efficiency, and security represents a considerable portion of the IT budget. Additionally, as technology rapidly evolves, there's a continuous need for upgrades and replacements, adding to the expenses.

3. Software and Cloud Services:

Licensing fees for essential software, subscriptions to cloud services, and support contracts are recurring expenses that can accumulate to a significant portion of the budget. The shift towards cloud computing, while offering scalability and flexibility, involves operational costs related to data storage, processing, and software-as-a-service (SaaS) subscriptions, which can be substantial depending on the size and needs of the business.

4. Compliance and Security:

With increasing threats from cyberattacks and the need for compliance with various regulatory standards (e.g., GDPR - General Data Protection Regulation in EU, HIPAA - Health Insurance Portability and Accountability Act , a US law), businesses must invest heavily in cybersecurity measures. This includes sophisticated security software, regular security audits, training for employees, and possibly hiring dedicated security personnel or consultants. The cost of ensuring data privacy and security is a significant and non-negotiable expense in the IT budget.

5. Human Capital:

Skilled IT professionals are in high demand and command high salaries. Investing in a talented workforce to manage, support, and innovate within the IT landscape is crucial. This includes not only the salaries but also benefits, training, and professional development to keep the skills of the IT staff up to date. Additionally, as IT projects become more complex and integral to every aspect of the business, the need for more specialized personnel increases, further driving up costs.

These factors combined underscore the strategic importance of the IT Budget for operational support, competitive advantage, and future growth. As technology continues to evolve and integrate more deeply into all aspects of business operations, the IT budget reflects both the opportunities and the necessities of this digital age.

Outline of this Chapter 8: Manage IT Budget

1. Effective IT budget management is crucial for aligning technological capabilities with organizational goals, ensuring optimal resource allocation.

2. A comprehensive understanding of both CAPEX and OPEX expenditures is essential for CIOs to navigate financial planning within the IT domain.

3. Proactive budget planning and regular review processes enable organizations to adapt to changing needs and market conditions efficiently.

4. Collaboration between IT and finance departments is vital for accurate forecasting and managing unexpected expenses within the allocated budget.

5. Continuous investment in digital transformation, infrastructure, software, security, and human capital is key to maintaining competitive advantage and supporting business growth.

Your records: I encourage you to write down your conclusion / ideas / actions from this Chapter. This action will ensure that the information you got will have practical utilization.

Chapter 9. Choosing the Right Project Management Methodology

In this chapter, I want to address an important subject: Project Management methodologies and which is best for your case.

Choosing the right project management methodology for specific projects is a critical responsibility for CIOs, as it significantly impacts the successful implementation of changes and projects, essential for company development.

A stable IT solution with excellent SLAs is insufficient for CIO responsibilities. If projects are not delivered on time, with the right quality, and using appropriate methodologies, it will pose a significant challenge for the company.

To start the selection of the right methodology and tools, CIOs need to consider which methodologies their team is familiar with, identify any issues with currently used methodologies for project implementation, and propose which methodology best suits each project.

Usually, the methodology of Project Management is part of PMO's responsibility. Hence, the CIO, responsible for project delivery, should closely cooperate with the PMO to adapt or change existing PM methodologies for the best efficiency and delivery.

Waterfall or Agile?

What I don't personally like is the usual presentation of Agile vs. Waterfall - many times it is considered in the following way: Agile is a new methodology, a more contemporary one, while Waterfall is an old methodology that is obsolete.

This interpretation is completely wrong.

It's important to understand that Waterfall and Agile are not competitors but complementary approaches, with some projects better suited to Waterfall and others to Agile.

Let's do a short review of each Methodology (information taken from standard PM manuals).

9.1 What Is The Waterfall Methodology?

The Waterfall methodology is a traditional project management approach that follows a linear and sequential design process. It is characterized by a strict phase-by-phase progression where each phase must be completed before the next one begins, with little to no overlap between phases.

In Picture 5 there is a representation of Waterfall methodology.

Picture 5. Diagram of Waterfall methodology

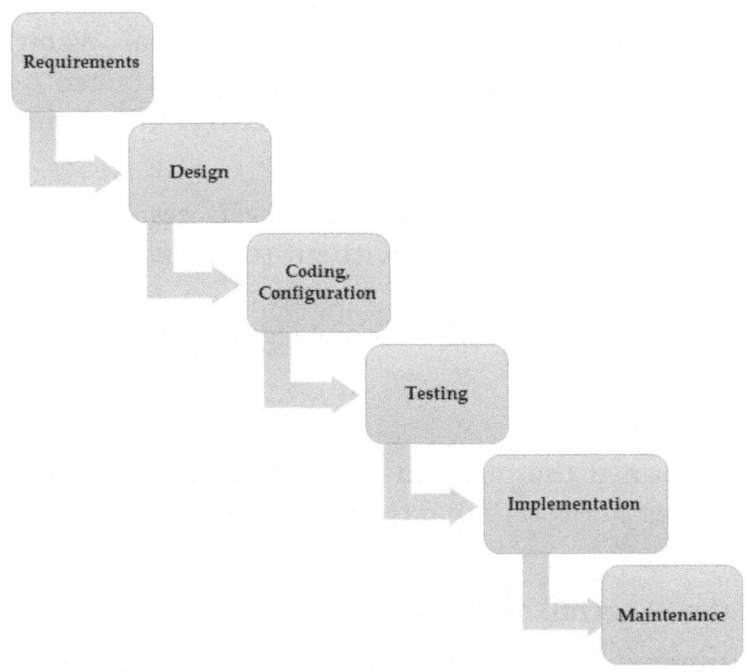

Key Characteristics of the Waterfall Methodology:

1. Sequential Phases: The Waterfall methodology divides the project into distinct phases such as Requirements, Design, Implementation (or Coding), Testing, Deployment, and Maintenance. Each phase relies on the deliverables of the previous phase and corresponds to a specialization of tasks.

2. Detailed Documentation: Because of its linear approach, the Waterfall methodology requires comprehensive documentation upfront. Each phase has its documentation requirements, ensuring a clear and detailed plan before moving on to the next phase.

3. Well-defined Objectives: The scope, timelines, and costs of the project are clearly defined at the beginning. This makes the Waterfall methodology suitable for projects with well-understood requirements that are unlikely to change during the development process.

4. Limited Client Involvement: In a traditional Waterfall project, client or end-user involvement is typically concentrated at the beginning (during requirement gathering) and at the end (during acceptance testing) of the project.

5. No Going Back: Once a phase has been completed, the project moves to the next phase without revisiting or revising the previous phases. This makes it difficult to accommodate changes or new requirements without significant rework and cost implications.

As we have learned the main characteristics of the Waterfall methodology, let's now see what the usual phases are.

Phases of the Waterfall Methodology:

1. Requirements: This initial phase involves gathering and documenting all specific requirements of the project, outlining what the end product should achieve.

2. Design: Based on the requirements, this phase involves creating the system design. It can be divided into two parts: high-level system architecture and detailed design.

3. Implementation (Configuration, Coding, Installation): During this phase, developers write code based on the previously defined design documentation.

4. Testing: Once the software is developed, it undergoes thorough testing to find and fix any defects or issues.

5. Deployment: After testing, the product is released to the production environment or delivered to the customer.

6. Maintenance: Post-deployment, this phase involves making updates, fixing bugs, and adding enhancements to ensure the product continues to meet user needs.

The Waterfall methodology is known for its simplicity and ease of management, particularly in projects with clear objectives and stable requirements. However, its rigidity can be a drawback in dynamic environments where requirements are subject to change.

9.2 What Is Agile Methodology?

Agile methodology is an iterative and incremental approach to project management and software development that helps teams deliver value to their customers faster and with fewer headaches.

In Picture 6 there is a representation of Agile methodology.

Picture 6. Diagram of Agile methodology.

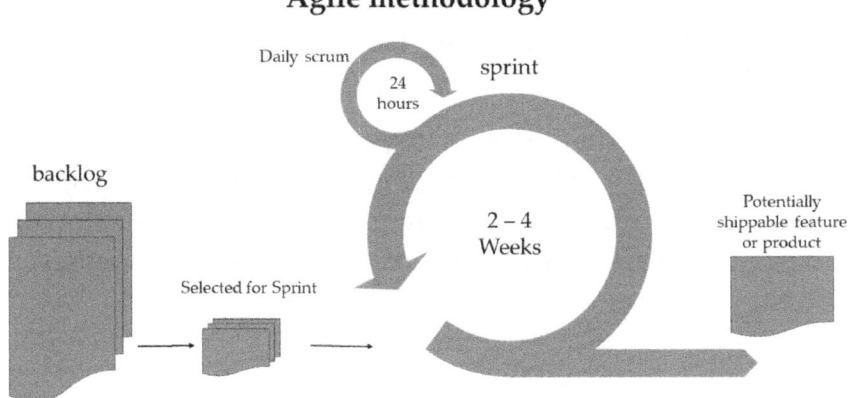

Key Characteristics of Agile Methodology are:

1. Iterative and Incremental Approach: Agile projects are divided into small, manageable units called iterations or sprints, which typically last between one to four weeks. Each iteration involves planning, designing, coding, and testing, resulting in a working product increment.

2. Customer Collaboration: Agile places a strong emphasis on customer involvement throughout the development process. Regular feedback is sought to ensure the product meets the customer's needs and expectations, allowing for adjustments as the project evolves.

3. Embrace Change: Agile methodologies welcome changing requirements, even late in development. Agile processes harness change for the customer's competitive advantage.

4. Cross-functional Teams: Agile projects are executed by self-organizing, cross-functional teams that collaborate closely. These teams encompass all the skills necessary to deliver product increments, from development to deployment.

5. Continuous Improvement: Agile methodologies encourage regular reflection on how to become more effective and then tuning and adjusting behavior accordingly. This applies to both the product and the process.

6. Simplicity: The art of maximizing the amount of work not done is essential. Agile methodologies emphasize simplicity and the importance of focusing on what's crucial to delivering value to the customer.

For CIOs, it is important to guide the PMO and IT team to choose the right methodology for a particular type of project: the key is "tailoring" the chosen methodology—Agile or Waterfall—to the project's needs and ensuring the project team fully understands the reasons behind the choice.

This involves a detailed consideration of project requirements, uncertainty levels, and the need for iterative development or a sequential approach.

Agile methodologies, characterized by sprints and iterative development, are recommended for projects with high uncertainty or those requiring frequent updates and functionality changes, like apps or platforms.

Conversely, projects with clear requirements and lower uncertainty levels may benefit more from the Waterfall methodology.

CIOs must ensure their teams are well-informed about the methodologies and possess the necessary skills to implement them effectively. This may involve training sessions, workshops, or bringing in external expertise.

Ultimately, the choice between Agile and Waterfall should not be seen as a binary one. Instead, CIOs should focus on selecting the best approach based on the specific needs of each project, even considering hybrid models that combine elements of both methodologies.

9.3 Which Methodology To Use?

At the end of the Chapter, I would like to show as a general guide which projects are using Agile and which Waterfall (within the IT scope):

Table 9. General guide for PM methodology usage.

Waterfall Projects	Agile Projects
Infrastructure Upgrades	**Software Development with Frequent Updates**
Upgrading network infrastructure or moving to a new data center requires careful planning and execution in a linear fashion.	Developing a web application or mobile app where features and requirements evolve based on user feedback.
Legacy System Migrations	**E-Commerce Platform Development**
Migrating from an old mainframe system to a modern platform needs detailed upfront planning to ensure data integrity and system compatibility.	Building and iterating on an e-commerce platform that needs to adapt quickly to changing market demands or consumer preferences.
Compliance and Regulatory Projects	**Customer Relationship Management (CRM) Systems**
Implementing systems or processes to meet new regulatory requirements often follows a strict sequence of steps to ensure compliance.	Developing or customizing CRM software to suit the dynamic needs of sales and marketing teams, requiring frequent updates.
Large-Scale Construction IT Projects	**Agile Software Development Projects**
Implementing IT	Projects that involve

infrastructure in new buildings or campuses, where the project scope and requirements are well-defined, and changes are minimal.	developing software solutions with iterative feedback loops, such as mobile applications or SaaS products.
ERP Implementations	**Digital Marketing Platforms**
Enterprise Resource Planning (ERP) system implementations are large and complex, requiring extensive planning and a phased rollout.	Creating and iterating on digital marketing platforms or campaigns that need to respond quickly to analytics and market trends.
Disaster Recovery Planning	**Prototype or MVP Development**
Developing and implementing disaster recovery plans for IT systems, where all steps need to be meticulously planned and documented.	Developing a prototype or Minimum Viable Product for a new tech product or service to validate concepts in a real-world environment quickly.
Hardware Deployments	**User Experience (UX) Projects**
Rolling out new hardware across an organization, such as servers or workstations, often requires a sequential approach to ensure compatibility and minimize disruptions.	Iterative design and testing of user interfaces for software products, where user feedback is integral to the development process.

Outline of Chapter 9: Choosing the Right Project Management Methodology

1. Critical Decision for CIOs: Avoid selecting a methodology solely based on external influences. Consider internal factors like the team's familiarity with methodologies, existing methodological challenges, and the suitability for specific projects. Offer ongoing support and training to enhance knowledge and practical skills.

2. Tailoring Methodologies (Waterfall, Agile, Hybrid): Ensure your team understands the core aspects of each methodology and involves them in choosing and customizing the most appropriate one for each project.

Your records: I encourage you to write down your conclusion / ideas / actions from this Chapter. This action will ensure that the information you get will have practical utilization.

Chapter 10. CIO Checklist
(bonus chapter)

As I stated at the beginning of the book, my goal was to provide a comprehensive and practical guide for any CIO. I believe that the methodologies presented in this book will equip you to not just manage but also enhance your role, leading to the successful achievement of broader organizational goals.

Here, I wanted to provide an additional tool, which can be referred to as the "CIO Checklist." This tool can be useful for examining your position from various angles and across different domains, and to identify any additional responsibilities that might fall under your purview.

CIO Checklist

A Chief Information Officer (CIO) plays a crucial role in aligning the IT strategy with the organization's goals and ensuring the efficient operation of IT services. Here's a comprehensive checklist that a CIO might use to manage their responsibilities effectively:

Strategic Planning

- Define IT strategic goals aligned with business objectives.

- Develop an IT roadmap for technology adoption and digital transformation.

- Conduct a SWOT analysis to identify strengths, weaknesses, opportunities, and threats in the IT landscape.

- Ensure IT governance frameworks are in place and compliant with industry standards.

Budget Management

- Prepare the IT budget, including CAPEX and OPEX, ensuring alignment with strategic goals.

- Implement cost-control measures to optimize spending.

- Monitor and report on IT spending against the budget regularly.

Cybersecurity and Compliance

- Assess and strengthen the organization's cybersecurity posture.

- Ensure compliance with relevant data protection regulations (e.g., GDPR, HIPAA).

- Develop and test incident response and disaster recovery plans.

Technology Management

- Oversee the management of IT infrastructure, ensuring reliability and scalability.

- Evaluate and implement new technologies to drive innovation and efficiency.

- Manage software and hardware lifecycle, from procurement to disposal.

Project and Portfolio Management

- Prioritize IT projects based on business impact and resource availability.

- Monitor project progress, ensuring they are delivered on time, within scope, and budget.

- Implement project management best practices and methodologies (e.g., Agile, Waterfall).

Vendor and Stakeholder Management

- Negotiate and manage contracts with IT vendors and service providers.

- Build strong relationships with key stakeholders, including business leaders and external partners.

- Ensure IT services meet or exceed expectations through SLAs and performance metrics.

Team Leadership and Development

- Foster a culture of innovation, collaboration, and continuous improvement within the IT team.

- Develop talent through training, mentorship, and career progression opportunities.

- Recruit and retain skilled IT professionals to fill key positions.

Performance Monitoring

- Implement IT KPIs and dashboards to monitor and report on IT performance.

- Conduct regular IT reviews and audits to identify areas for improvement.

- Adjust IT strategies and operations based on performance data and feedback.

Risk Management

- Identify IT risks related to security, data privacy, and technology obsolescence.

- Implement risk mitigation strategies and regularly review risk assessments.

- Ensure business continuity through robust risk management practices.

Innovation and Digital Transformation

- Foster a culture that encourages innovation and experimentation.

- Lead digital transformation initiatives to improve customer experience and operational efficiency.

- Stay abreast of industry trends and emerging technologies that could impact the organization.

IT Service Management

- Ensure ITIL/ITSM (Information Technology Infrastructure Library / IT Service Management) processes are in place for effective IT service delivery.

- Monitor service desk performance to improve user satisfaction and reduce downtimes.

- Implement continuous service improvement processes to enhance IT service quality.

This checklist can help CIOs ensure they are covering the critical aspects of their role.

It should be adapted to fit the specific needs and context of your organization.

Conclusion

Navigating the role of a Technology leader within a company is undeniably challenging. On the one hand, you must actively engage with the business's strategic challenges, while on the other, you are tasked with maintaining the seamless operation of all technology components and ensuring that your technology team is equipped to foster both growth and stability.

I believe this book serves as your guide through the complexities of Technology Management.

I will add here what I wrote at the beginning - all the real-life cases presented are genuine, with minor modifications made solely to eliminate any confidential elements. My primary objective was to share authentic examples from real-life situations without causing harm to anyone. Building a foundation rooted in practical experience is essential, and that is precisely what I aim to provide.

I invite you to share your thoughts, feedback, and requests for additional content. I am eager to enhance, modify, and furnish you with more practical information that will empower you to excel in your role effectively.

You can contact me here:

LinkedIn – https://www.linkedin.com/in/radu-spataru

X (twitter.com) - https://twitter.com/RaduSpataru3

Website – https://ingines.pro , https://spataruradu.gumroad.com

Abbreviations used in this book.

Abbreviation	Full Form/Description
CIO	Chief Information Officer (CIO) holds a pivotal role in managing an organization's information technology strategy and infrastructure. This position is akin to roles such as IT Director or Head of IT.
CTO	Chief Technical Officer or Chief Technology Officer (CTO) is a leadership position responsible for overseeing the technological aspects of a company. While in some companies, the role may be like CIO, in specific domains like Telecom or Development-oriented companies, distinctions exist.
SMART	SMART is a method employed to articulate Objectives and Key Performance Indicators (KPIs) with clarity. The acronym stands for Specific, Measurable, Achievable, Relevant, and Time-bound. This methodology ensures that goals are well-defined, quantifiable, realistic, aligned with broader objectives, and have specific timeframes for accomplishment.
SLA	Service Level Agreement (SLA) is a

	contractual arrangement between a service provider and a customer. It outlines the expected level of service, including quality, availability, and the responsibilities of each party. SLAs are commonly utilized in various industries, including information technology, telecommunications, and business process outsourcing.
CAPEX	Capital Expenditure (CAPEX) refers to the funds a company invests in acquiring, upgrading, or maintaining physical assets. These investments are made with the expectation of generating future benefits for the organization. CAPEX is distinct from Operational Expenditure (OPEX) as it involves long-term asset-related investments.
OPEX	Operational Expenditure (OPEX) encompasses the ongoing costs incurred by a business in its day-to-day operations to sustain its essential functions. These expenses include utilities, rent, salaries, maintenance, and other operational costs. In contrast to CAPEX, which involves long-term investments, OPEX is associated with regular, short-term costs crucial for daily business activities.
RFP	Request for Proposal (RFP) is a formal

	document created by an organization to solicit bids or proposals from qualified vendors or service providers for a specific project or service. The RFP outlines project requirements, scope of work, expected deliverables, and relevant details, providing a structured approach for organizations to communicate their needs and evaluate detailed proposals from potential suppliers.
RFI	An RFI (request for information) is a formal process for gathering information from potential suppliers of a good or service.
SPOC	Single point of contact - key person responsible for a domain and / or project. If this person is responsible for a project inside IT, she or he can easily get the status, escalate and / or help the internal team excel in this project
PMO	Project Management Office - team or position of person(s) responsible for Projects management process inside the company.
GDPR	The General Data Protection Regulation (GDPR) is a comprehensive data protection law that became enforceable on May 25, 2018, in the European Union (EU). It sets guidelines for the collection, processing, and storage of personal information of individuals within the EU and the European Economic Area (EEA). The GDPR

	aims to give individuals more control over their personal data and to harmonize data privacy laws across Europe.
HIPAA	The Health Insurance Portability and Accountability Act (HIPAA) is a US law enacted in 1996, designed to protect the privacy and security of individuals' medical information and ensure health insurance coverage for workers and their families when they change or lose their jobs. HIPAA establishes national standards for electronic healthcare transactions, healthcare providers, health plans, and other entities that process health information.
E2E	End to End approach
DR	Disaster Recovery (DR) in the IT domain refers to a set of policies, tools, and procedures that enable the recovery or continuation of vital technology infrastructure and systems following a natural or human-induced disaster.
BC	Business Continuity (BC) refers to the processes, policies, and procedures that enable an organization to maintain essential functions or quickly resume them in the event of a major disruption, whether due to natural disasters, cyber-attacks, or other significant threats.
ITIL	Information Technology Infrastructure Library: ITIL is a set of detailed practices for IT service management (ITSM) that focuses on aligning IT services with the

	needs of business. It provides a practical framework for identifying, planning, delivering, and supporting IT services to the business.
ITSM	IT Service Management: ITSM refers to the entirety of activities, policies, and processes that organizations use to design, deliver, manage, and improve the IT services provided to customers. It's oriented towards the effective and efficient delivery of IT services to support business objectives.
CMDB	Configuration Management Database - A CMDB provides a common place to store data associated with IT assets and configuration items.
SWOT	SWOT analysis (or SWOT matrix) is a strategic planning and strategic management technique used to help a person or organization identify Strengths, Weaknesses, Opportunities, and Threats related to business competition or project planning.

List of Diagrams and Tables

Picture 1: We are busy ... to do the transformation. (Chapter 1)

Picture 2. Backup and Handover process. (Chapter "C")

Picture 3. Example of Business and IT strategy on one slide. (Chapter 3, point 3.5)

Picture 4. Example IT Strategy Execution Roadmap on 2 slides. (Chapter 4)

Picture 5. Diagram of Waterfall methodology (Chapter 9, point 9.1)

Picture 6. Diagram of Agile methodology. (Chapter 9, point 9.2)

Table 1. IT assessment template (Chapter 2)

Table 2. Example of Information Categorization. (Chapter 5, point 5.2)

Table 3. Core differences between Business Continuity and Disaster Recovery. (Chapter 5, point 5.7)

Table 4. Salary Grid Example. (Chapter 6, point 6.3)

Table 5. Example of SWOT analysis - select the IT tool X (Chapter 7, point 7.3)

Table 6. Example of IT KPIs. (Chapter 7, point 7.7)

Table 7. IT Budget - CAPEX. (Chapter 8, point 8.3)

Table 8. IT Budget - OPEX. (Chapter 8, point 8.3)

Table 9. General guide for PM methodology usage. (Chapter 9, point 9.3)

References

Quotes used in the Book.

1. "Today's IT leaders need to be business leaders first, with a strong understanding of the organization's strategic goals, market context, and business processes." Jill Dyche - from the book "The New IT: How Technology Leaders are Enabling Business Strategy in the Digital Age" by the same author, is a book that discusses the evolving role of IT in organization.

2. "Productivity is meaningless unless you know what your goal is." by Eliyahu M. Goldratt and Jeff Cox – from the Book "The Goal: A Process of Ongoing Improvement" by Eliyahu M. Goldratt and Jeff Cox is a seminal work in the field of operations management and business efficiency.

3. "Ideas are easy. Execution is everything." by John Doerr – from the Book "Measure What Matters" by John Doerr is a book that emphasizes the importance of goal-setting and focus in organizations.

4. "The CIO Paradox is a set of contradictions that lies at the core of IT leadership. The paradox encapsulates the daily challenges that CIOs face, and it is what makes the role so difficult, and so interesting." by Martha Heller – from the Book "The CIO Paradox: Battling the Contradictions of IT Leadership" by Martha Heller provides valuable insights into the challenges and paradoxes faced by Chief Information Officers (CIOs) in the rapidly evolving field of information technology.

5. "Productivity is meaningless unless you know what your goal is." – by Eliyahu M. Goldratt and Jeff Cox – from the Book "The Goal: A Process of Ongoing Improvement" by Eliyahu M. Goldratt and Jeff Cox is a seminal work in the field of operations management and business efficiency

6. "Approximately 75% of venture-backed startups fail. The number is difficult to pin down, and some estimates suggest it could be even higher." Elizabeth Pollman, University of Pennsylvania, in the study about reasons of Startup Failure.

ABOUT THE AUTHOR

Radu Spataru

After spending numerous years as an IT expert in various domains, my professional journey has been characterized by continual growth and a steadfast commitment to driving positive change.

As I advanced from being an expert to taking on management roles, including Team Leader, IT Manager, Project Manager, and eventually CIO/CTO/CEO, each new position offered not only better salary and conditions but also a host of challenges. This transition required a significant shift in my thinking; I realized that I couldn't tackle tasks in the same manner as before, even with my superior understanding of the work and processes. New management responsibilities surfaced, encompassing budgeting, team leadership, conflict resolution, and more.

With nearly two decades of experience in Technology Management, I became inspired to distill the valuable insights I had acquired over the years into clear and concise guides, aiming to share them with others.